Don't Quit Your Day Job

THE
CORPORATE ENTREPRENEUR

ROBERT GERHARD

outskirts
press

The Corporate Entrepreneur
All Rights Reserved.
Copyrigkt © 2022 Robert Gerhard
v4.0

The opinions expressed in this manuscript are solely the opinions of the author and do not represent the opinions or thoughts of the publisher. The author has represented and warranted full ownership and/or legal right to publish all the materials in this book.

This book may not be reproduced, transmitted, or stored in whole or in part by any means, including graphic, electronic, or mechanical without the express written consent of the publisher except in the case of brief quotations embodied in critical articles and reviews.

Outskirts Press, Inc.
http://www.outskirtspress.com

ISBN: 978-1-9772-5500-6

Cover Photo © 2022 www.gettyimages.com. All rights reserved - used with permission.

Outskirts Press and the "OP" logo are trademarks belonging to Outskirts Press, Inc.

PRINTED IN THE UNITED STATES OF AMERICA

Table of Contents

Introduction V

1. A New Way of Life 1
2. Important Choices 8
3. Choosing and Motivating Managers 23
4. Your CPA, Your Lawyer,
   and Your Personal Assistant 29
5. The CEO in the Mirror 35
6. Knowing Your Limitations 42
7. Paying the Price 50
8. Distributorships 57
9. Minding the Store 64
10. The Virtual World 71
11. Discipline and Tenacity 77
12. Business Partners 83
13. Schadenfreude 87
14. Adapting to New Environments 92
15. Lessons Learned 97

*To my family, friends, and dogs
I've had both past and present.
Also, to my younger self,
without your unwavering
discipline and tenacity,
it couldn't have been done.*

Introduction

AS A SALES consultant in the Big Pharma industry, I was attending one of our company's "Plan of Action" meetings early one morning at the Admirals Club facility on the tenth floor of the local Marriott hotel. We sat down and one of my colleagues, Steven (a fictitious name, like all the names in this book) spotted me. I was busily working on one of my side enterprises, organizing my swing trades. I've always been interested in and involved in the stock market. Steven asked me, "Hey, what are you doing?" Prior times when we had met and he had seen me working on my real estate investments or other business endeavors, he confided in me that he was very unhappy with his current job. So when he walked in on me at the Marriott, he sat down, and I shared with him some of the concepts of what I call "the corporate entrepreneur." Truth be told, at first Steven was shocked by the extent of the various enterprises and businesses my wife and I currently owned. His first and most puzzling question was: "Why are you still at your current job?"

My explanation, at least to me, seemed obvious. I asked him, "What could be better than to go into a venture with most of your expenses already covered by your present job?"

He furrowed his brow and replied, "What do you mean?"

I explained that most first-time business ventures fail because of lack of cash, or cash flow, or both. In other words, it is difficult to cover your own daily domestic expenses when your new business is not yet off the ground.

"Think about it," I said. "By keeping my current job, I have a company car, an expense account, and benefits. These things provide me with more than enough ability to run my side businesses."

I could see the twinge on Steven's face, as if to say, "Sure, everybody can do that too!" I could tell that he was skeptical, yet curious how I am able to pull this off. I can't be sure, but I suspect that he may have even been a bit envious, too, when he heard all that I had going for myself on the side even while I was earning my salary and receiving benefits.

We had more discussions over the years, and I would explain to him about my businesses and that things were going fantastic. I guess I eventually got through to him. He loosened up and told me he was thinking of buying a farm in Iowa, and the last I heard, Steven had not only purchased that farm, but he'd also transformed it into a lucrative hazelnut operation. All without quitting his day job!

I've written this book because I believe that you too could benefit from what I want to share with you. Are you working for a company and doing OK for yourself, but you're still falling short of your financial goals? Are you ready to rise to new heights? This book and the principles that I teach in it are for people on the lookout for opportunities, the kind of folks willing to try something new and different to build a better life for themselves and their family.

Here are some of Steve's questions that I answered for him:

How can one do this while not quitting your day job? How and where do you find the time? Is being a corporate entrepreneur right for me?

We will go into all the details later in the book, but for now, just let me say that if you are like me, making the time for your side business ventures is not going to be as difficult as you might think. You are going to find the time while driving to work, when you would otherwise be cruising social media, or on your lunch break (instead of gossiping about what is going on at the company where you work!).

It involves the wise use of time rather than wasting time. Another inevitable (and very reasonable) question is: How much money do I need to get started in a new enterprise? That depends on what you're going to be delving into.

Take me for example. One of my first ventures was to become a wrist watch distributor. It didn't take much or any money for me to get started. As a distributor, the manufacturers were more than happy to give me free samples so I could show them to stores. I landed over fifty accounts. The only money that changed hands was sales to me. I simply used my time wisely.

With enough ambition, even the "average person" can no doubt make this work. You'd be surprised how motivational it is to know that your extra efforts will result in enjoying a better lifestyle while securing your financial future.

There's no substitute for good role models. And if you don't have one, that's okay; keep reading and you will learn from my experiences. When I was a kid, I saw my father, who was a German immigrant with a machinist job, get involved in what we know today as "flipping houses." That is buying derelict houses for a favorable price, rehabbing them, and selling them for a big profit.

I remember my father would go to work and then contact my mother, keeping her updated so she could tend to business functions such as bookkeeping and paperwork. I recall taking a bus with my mom to the brokerage companies in downtown Omaha and getting a check for fifteen to twenty thousand dollars—and this was back in the '70s, so adjust that for inflation into today's dollars and you will see how well Dad was doing for himself! Meanwhile, all I heard from my friends was how their parents were constantly rubbing two nickels together to try to get by. We never saw anything like that in my house, and that is when the entrepreneurial seed was planted.

Still, I didn't set out to be an entrepreneur. I have a marketing degree and an MBA as well. I set out to be a sales and marketing professional as my primary career, and I've been very successful at it. But I've also ended up doing what I saw and admired so much as a kid.

My first job out of college was working in sales for an office equipment manufacturer. At the same time, I got involved with my father in house flipping on the investment side. Some of the homes we bought as rental properties forty years ago I still own today, and they are still making us money. I liked the real estate business and its day-to-day routine. Meanwhile, I was making six figures on my primary job.

I am sometimes asked, why not just put all of your efforts within the company you work for and rise up through the ranks? There are several reasons. For one, a promotion often means you have to move to another location, quite possibly clear across the country. You don't have that problem as an entrepreneur. Wherever your businesses are located, you can operate them (and hire out people to help them function) right from where you currently live and work. No need to uproot yourself and your entire family every few years!

America truly is the land of opportunity—that's not just some cliché. And if your ambition is to acquire extra wealth and enjoy the challenges of entrepreneurship, your adventure is just beginning. The corporate entrepreneur truly lives with one foot in the best of both worlds. One of these days your friends will come and ask how you did it, how did you become so successful in business while continuing with your career? You will just smile and tell them, "It all started one day when I heard about this great new book..."

Ask me anything, robertgerhard77@gmail.com. I do webinars, seminars, speaker's programs plus one-on-one consulting sessions...all tailor made for you!

CHAPTER 1

A New Way of Life

IF YOU EVER hope to become a successful corporate entrepreneur, you must first have the right mindset. The key traits of this are ambition, motivation, and organization. You also have to be willing to take risks. I don't mean risks as in gambling or something reckless, but a willingness to seize opportunities when they present themselves—only, of course, after ample due diligence. Yes, to some degree you are going to be putting yourself out on a limb with any new business endeavor. However, you should never let that put a brake on your ambitions, as there is no substitute for the tenacity that comes with always keeping your eyes open for your next prospective venture.

This zeal for new horizons, however, often leads to the common misperception that what motivates corporate entrepreneurs is dissatisfaction with their current job or career path. After all, many ask, isn't this something that you do only because you're at the end of your rope at the workplace? My answer is an emphatic no! In fact, the better, more stable your day job, the better your chance of success, because you are operating from a basis of strength and have a firm anchor.

Your age and your current profession should never hold you back from becoming a corporate entrepreneur; the only prerequisite is the desire to greatly improve your financial situation through wise business dealings while maintaining your current employment.

The corporate entrepreneur is a go-getter who time after time exhibits the stamina and ability to operate various businesses simultaneously, which involves multitasking, to say the least. It's well worth the effort, though, because you don't want to limit yourself to just any one venture at a time. Throw away your fear of failure.

Now, before going any further, let me briefly touch on an important topic. When you first start getting involved in sideline businesses you are going to be tempted to start telling other people—including those with whom you work—about the exciting new things going on in your life. Well, fight off those temptations! No matter how much you may believe you can trust people, think how fast "office gossip" spreads. And what if you should have a falling-out with one of your colleagues? For these reasons, I strongly advise that you keep your extracurricular businesses strictly confidential or at least exercise extreme caution in deciding with whom to share any details. If your day job bosses know about it, they are not going to like it, so it's best they don't know. There is no benefit to them to your spending any amount of time on your personal business activities, let alone the suspicion they might have of you working your own business on *their* time. Anybody who thinks otherwise is living in a dream world.

There is nothing unethical about being a corporate entrepreneur. This is a free country, and you are at liberty to operate and participate within the free enterprise system as much as you wish. Nonetheless, as the old saying goes, discretion is the better part of valor, so a wise person holds their cards close to the vest as much as possible.

Here's a cautionary tale that vividly illustrates my point. A woman I know who works in a position similar to mine decided one day that she wanted to continue to work at her job and go to law school at the same time. The natural implication is that upon graduation she probably is not going to stay with the company. She shared her new educational aspirations with some of her friends at the office, who then promptly told managers. This ambitious woman soon received an ultimatum. Even though the law school isn't a business, she was educating herself to get into a different business: the law business. Her bosses told her that she could either continue working at her day job and quit law school or continue going to law school and quit her day job. She ended staying with the day job. But it's a choice she would have never been forced to make if she had only kept her plans to herself.

Of course, by the same token, there are people in your life with whom you most certainly do want to share your corporate entrepreneur plans; and in fact, these are the people who can help you to accomplish them. An ideal situation would be a spouse, friend, or relative—in other words, people you can deeply trust, and who might end up taking part in your business activities, which will benefit both of you.

Seek out those who may have interests or talents that would be beneficial for your endeavors. For example, my wife has always been very interested in physical fitness, and that is one of the reasons we made the decision to get into the health club business as one of our sidelines. She is also a phenomenal interior designer, so not only is she involved with hiring people for our health club, but she is in charge of developing the interior design, too. Always be on the lookout for synergies. That's an important factor when you are putting together your team. I consider my wife a team captain. Good friends might also fit in that role. We will discuss this in more detail in a later chapter.

Above all, try to avoid naysayers, whoever they may be (this can include close family members). If they are always negative and saying it can't be done, they are more than not helpful; they can be downright toxic to your plans of succeeding as a corporate entrepreneur. There are people out there who will read this book and say, "It can't be done." Well, I'm living proof that it can be done, with a good solid plan and the stick-to-itiveness to turn your plans into reality.

Here is a key piece of the puzzle: it is crucial that you maintain the ability to do your day job while still being able to check on your team members to get something done that has to be done. That means there has to be a good deal of well-thought-out coordination between you and your team. At the very least, you should probably have your spouse or close friends involved. However, this is only possible once you get yourself into the habit and mindset of staying extremely well-organized. I strongly recommend that you utilize a checklist to maximize earning potential. This will help you keep track of everything that needs to be done at your current position. You should also start writing a daily business journal for all your businesses and see what tactics and strategies worked for you and which did not. A goal checklist for every day is likewise indispensable, because you're going to be interweaving your day job and your various business enterprises on a continuous basis.

You have to be sure to accomplish everything on your "day job checklist" as efficiently as possible. After all, your day job is the mainstay and foundation of your primary career. As such, it is what affords you the opportunity to pursue becoming a corporate entrepreneur in the first place. Compare your situation with entrepreneurs who do not have the "safety net" of a day job. What an added burden! They have to not only worry about surviving in their business pursuits, but they also must be able to sustain their home and personal expenses based on the fortunes of their business. If things go wrong, even temporarily, they might have real trouble paying the bills some months. As a corporate entrepreneur, so long as you do nothing to jeopardize your day job, you will never experience that dreaded sinking feeling in your stomach wondering how you are going to make ends meet.

So you will have to work not just smartly but efficiently, because you have to keep a good performance in your current gig in order to support your entrepreneurial ventures. If you do your day job well and can get through by three o'clock in the afternoon, you should have that time available to work at your entrepreneurial endeavors. This is even easier for those who work in the field in sales positions, and those who work in an office will have to be more careful.

The more outside ventures you are involved with, the imperative to become highly organized gets even more pronounced. By that point, however, you should be making enough money to pay an assistant to work fifteen to thirty hours a week to help you stay on task. An assistant can relieve you of all the little details that will hold you back from expanding your business horizons even further. There is so much minutiae that goes into chores such as dealing with CPAs and vendors (and a million other details), but a dependable assistant, once trained, can take care of all of this.

The best way to find an assistant could be a neighborhood blog, or perhaps through Craigslist ads. You would be looking for someone who has had office experience, is a whiz at organization, and somebody who is willing to work according to the schedule that you need. He or she has to be trainable and willing to work and be happy with about fifteen to twenty dollars per hour. You should interview five candidates before you hire someone. An independent contractor situation is best, at least at first. That way you don't need to get involved with payroll taxes or be responsible for overtime or other perks. Of course, if they get good enough at the job, you might consider that it is to your advantage to eventually take them on board with your organization as a regular employee.

Now we are coming to the crucial question of what kind of business venture should you try to get things started? For one thing, don't think that you necessarily have to restrict yourself to any particular geographic region. For example, I have owned a number of businesses in my native Midwest while living in Florida. I choose businesses by how easy they are to operate, something where my presence isn't required. I like the Midwest because the people seem to be a tad more honest, and the rate of unemployment is low.

That is how things have worked out for me. For you, it might involve very different areas of the country, or perhaps seeking opportunities outside of the United States. That's one of the most powerful benefits of becoming a corporate entrepreneur. Where you currently reside has no bearing on your prospects for success. The entire world is quite literally well within your reach. Technology has helped to "shrink" the world, and conducting business is no longer like it was in the old days, when your actual physical presence was almost always required. That only makes sense, because the business is not depending on your body or your physical labor. Instead, it is your brain that matters, the smart choices that you make, your ability to lead your businesses as you build them up, and your unswerving dedication to giving every new thing that you try your best effort and maximum commitment.

Whether you own a business down the street or in another corner of the globe, the principles of what it takes to be a successful corporate entrepreneur will never change. And technology has done a great job of bridging the gap, no matter how many miles exist between you and your business. Once you realize that, you've now broadened the possibilities of a better way of life for you and your family in ways that you may have never dreamed would be possible—and in fact to a large degree were not possible up until just a few years ago. Be glad you live in this modern era—it was tailor-made for the corporate entrepreneur.

What is most vital to remember, however, is that you need to keep your eyes peeled for situations that fit your own particular circumstances and settings that make you comfortable. Remember, if you so choose, you can be a corporate entrepreneur for the rest of your life, so of course you will want play to your strengths and enjoy what you are doing every step of the way. In the next chapter, we're going to find out a lot more about how you can best make all the crucial decisions that lie ahead.

CHAPTER 2

Important Choices

NOW COMES THE fun part! Yes, you have at this point made the momentous decision that you do indeed want to live the life of a corporate entrepreneur, but precisely what line of business should you pursue first? There is not a "one size fits all" answer to that. Making the right choices involves some solid analysis and a good deal of introspection, thinking about what kinds of sidelines you might enjoy and that would interest you. You need to create a "wish list" of your favorite types of business, the kinds of ventures that would line up with both your interests and your abilities.

Here's a good real-world example. I had a medical device representative who worked for me during my three years as the national sales director of a medical devices company. As I was good friends with her and her husband, I confided in her that I had sideline businesses. She was intrigued and told me that while she enjoys what she's doing, she too would like to branch out and possibly start some other business. When I discovered that she hadn't graduated from college yet and had a little school left, I made a suggestion. I told her that the best thing she could do is get her degree and finish the last semester.

She was my number one person in the South, a very judicious individual and multifaceted. She came to me and we had a mutual understanding that she was going to go back to school and during that time she would decide what outside business opportunity she would like to pursue. So she finished her school, and I even sent letters of recommendation to her professors. During that same time period, we held numerous discussions. I learned that she had a great deal of enthusiasm for real estate sales. She had never contemplated going into real estate on the side, but I strongly encouraged her to follow through on her dreams.

She took my advice, and while continuing in her day job career, she now also maintains a lucrative sideline managing her real estate investments. My friend had always harbored an interest in real estate, but now she is using that interest as a very productive way of earning extra money. She has also (as was suggested in the last chapter) enlisted the help of her husband and they presently own five rental homes. He has just recently become involved in flipping homes that have "heritage value." These are homes that a local historical board has deemed as historically significant, usually with a plaque displayed prominently somewhere near the front door. As we briefly mentioned in the Introduction, flipping homes is generally described as when you buy distressed real estate (foreclosures, estate sales, etc.), put in some work rehabilitating it, and then sell it for a much higher price than you had paid for it. This additional sideline has taken their real estate business to a whole new level.

My friend is a perfect example of a corporate entrepreneur who, with the help of her spouse, has taken something that she always had a passion for (but had never actively pursued) transformed it into a thriving business enterprise, earning significant extra income for her family, along with enormous personal satisfaction. It all begins when you imagine what you want to achieve—more than money, look deep down. Is this something that you are going to be able to juggle, and where do you want to be in the near future? What will you and your family look like five years from now? Do you want to be financially secure and potentially debt free? Does economic freedom excite you? What else does it make you want to achieve? This may be a great chance for what always had been a pipe dream to become your new reality.

When you're selecting a sideline business, you can't choose something where you have to be physically present most of the time. For the most part, you will be operating your businesses remotely. For example, you can do teleconferences during your lunch hour. You can also do them on your daily commute both to and from work. Ever see people stuck in traffic jams with their cell phones at their ear? For a corporate entrepreneur, it can be a lot more productive and profitable than talking about Monday night's football game. Don't text or check your e-mail while you're driving, of course, but these days there are lots of voice-activated systems where technology allows you to do so hands-free.

You can also use time zone difference to your advantage. For example, if you're in Florida and your businesses are in the Midwest, you can be done with your day job work in Florida at five (or earlier) and then still have an "extra" hour to devote to your own business. If your corporate entrepreneur ventures are in California, you have a three-hour time zone difference, which affords even greater flexibility.

TAKE OVER A TURNKEY OPERATION.

When it comes to what types of business you should consider, some people prefer a "turnkey" operation. This is where you literally open the front door and you are all set to start doing business that day. You are ready to go. This is usually a currently operating business that you are buying from the owner. He or she is going to retire, is too sick to operate it, or has nobody to turn it over to.

CREATE A STARTUP.

The alternative is a business where you build it from the ground up. Buy or lease space, stock it, do the advertising, hire the help, decide on a name, design ads—everything you need to run a successful business. The comparative costs and your time available to do all the above can help you to decide which is better for you.

BECOME A FRANCHISEE.

You will also want to consider a franchise business. Much has been written about franchises, and the success stories are legend. You enjoy significant advantages over mom-and-pop operations in that you have immediate brand recognition, along with numerous other benefits. On the flip side, of course, you do give up some control over your own business to the franchisor. It is somewhat of a trade-off that you need to factor into the equation. We will examine all this in much more detail later in the book.

An important aspect of going into or acquiring any business is that you have to look at markets you are familiar with in the US and overseas. I have had businesses in Mexico and

Jamaica that are easy to communicate with and have worked out well for me. That, of course, is part of due diligence. You never want to get involved with a business that you know absolutely nothing about. Nonetheless, even if you are interested in a business in which your knowledge is somewhat limited, don't necessarily dismiss it out of hand. You can study, research, and learn a lot about the field in a relatively short period of time. As we mentioned previously, ideally it should be a situation where you don't have to be physically present and you can be involved in a remote way. A good example would be the storage business. What's nice about storage complexes like those that I own and operate is that it is both real estate and a retail business, so that you get all the advantages of both. Moreover, this business involves very little overhead, though you most definitely need a highly qualified and reliable manager.

Also, you have to give careful consideration to whether or not to go into business with an outside partner (someone who is not a close family member). I will share with you one of my first ventures, the aforementioned storage business. I wound up in this business more or less by default. We started out getting a great piece of land on which we were going to build a convenience store/restaurant. But the partner I had in mind couldn't come to the table with any money. He also had bad credit and had made some poor business choices. But we didn't find that out till later. He had come to us because I had done a prior small venture with him in the tree business, but this time, things didn't work out so well. When the proposed deal fell through, he actually tried to sue us for breach of contract. File this one under the heading of choosing bad or undesirable business partners.

The scenario started out with us learning that a choice three acres was for sale. This man came to us (my wife and I) and tried to convince us that the best chance of success would be to open a convenience store and restaurant. He would be part owner and operate the business. It all fell apart when we learned that we did not have proper access to the lot for vehicle traffic and parking, and that the proposed venture could not possibly succeed as a retail location. Therefore, we had to terminate our relationship with this man. We had a contract and a loose operating agreement on which he then successfully sued for breach of contract and won a substantial judgment. We appealed and finally won out in a Supreme Court of Iowa decision where his judgment was overturned. We then basically developed the land as a storage complex, and it has become one of our most successful properties to date. Here's a perfect example of two things. Make sure your contract is ironclad and in your favor, and also *choose the right partner*. Moreover, you always want to be the primary partner.

Not only that, but you have to really immerse yourself into the industry you are considering before delving into it, as you never want to do so without first acquiring the requisite background knowledge. For example, my wife and I attended numerous seminars and we talked to the biggest gurus in the US about the storage business. We read every book possible with regards to the business. We actually developed ourselves to become experts in the business. We took the attitude of fake it till you make it! That process took about eighteen months. We were also quite cognizant that this would involve an investment of about $250,000.

There are other situations where you are not necessarily looking for a business partner (hopefully not because my story scared you off!), but you need somebody who is going to be involved with your new enterprise to a larger extent than simply being an employee. This is an approach that I have used successfully, for example, in the health club business. One of the great advantages of this field is that there are a lot of twenty-something males and females who are incredibly well versed who would love to be a manager or someone to whom you could give some "sweat equity." (No, I'm not talking about the perspiration that comes from working out at the club.) Seriously, this is where you offer them some share of the business in return for the work and commitment that they are willing to put into making it a success. You can set certain goals and milestones for them that will be tied to their compensation and the stake in the company you are willing to offer them. Such young go-getters invariably are thrilled to be able to have an opportunity to run the day-to-day operations, which should give you much peace of mind that business is being carried on in the right way. It is an exceptionally easy business for the corporate entrepreneur to run by remote control.

While you could start a health club from scratch, research has proven that the franchise concept has much more chance for success. Your best bet would be to pick one of the better franchises and run with it. Yes, you could try competing on your own with no franchise affiliation, but the odds are highly likely that national brand recognition would be too hard to overcome, and you wouldn't be able to effectively compete.

A boutique club is a fitness facility that generally may be anywhere from five to ten thousand square feet. They concentrate on aerobic and Zumba-type classes. They also do stationary bicycles and treadmills. Many have a small area where a personal trainer might take clients for workouts on a one-on-one basis. These clubs tend to be good moneymakers, especially depending on whether you lease or rent the building. Your start-up costs would generally be at least $350,000 or so.

Overall, the health club business is on everybody's top ten list of sideline ventures. For those who don't have access to that kind of money, there are countless other businesses that you can explore that are less costly when it comes to the initial investment. A good example would be sandwich franchises, such as Firehouse Subs, Subway, and many others. In these types of franchises, you have to make sure that you hire a manager who you would give some 'sweat equity' in return—which, as described earlier, involves giving the person you've put in charge of operations a share of the profits, as well as a salary. In this case, the person would not charge you for overtime or other work-related benefits. His or her primary goal would be to make a success of the business and to share in that success. He or she would naturally have to be someone you implicitly trust and whom you feel supremely confident would do a good job.

When it comes to sandwich shops, starting off locally probably makes the most sense. Why? Well, for one thing, you would be able to supervise what is going on at the shop on a personal level, dropping in (often unexpectedly) for a visit whenever you wanted, to check things out; so you have the best of both possible worlds! While you are not involved in the day-to-day operations per se, you can keep a close eye on how the business is doing and be a presence that the employees would respect. It's a great way to incentivize everyone there to do their job and to do it the right way, too.

BECOME A DISTRIBUTOR.

Here's another top of the list idea, that may just become one of your first corporate entrepreneur businesses: become a distributor for an overseas company with no US distribution, but with a strong desire to expand into the coveted American marketplace. You'd be developing a sales team and a supply team that would market and sell products for that manufacturer. This would require a good deal of market research before you make your first move, but your efforts could pay off big-time if you play your cards right.

I have been a distributor from everything from wrist watches to cowboy boots. It doesn't necessarily have to be products that you are personally interested in, though I think that certainly helps, especially when it comes to familiarity with the merchandise and the motivation to sell it as vigorously as possible.

NEW PRODUCT DEVELOPMENT, MARKETING, AND DISTRIBUTION.

Another great potential corporate entrepreneur business might be to develop and distribute a new product on your own. A friend of mine did this by bringing over an innovative exercise product from Hong Kong. He placed ads in *Sports Illustrated* and the sports section of newspapers nationwide and probably sold fifty thousand of them. And I've seen other novel ideas, for example, a fresh flower vending machine for hospitals that had been developed in Germany. Think of the potential of that idea, walking into a hospital room and hand-delivering fresh flowers! I think it beats the impersonal delivery by a florist's driver. Set your sights high, but remain realistic. It doesn't have to be a product that revolutionizes an industry or changes consumers' way of life. Just buy into something new and different that has potential.

This was back in the '80s, and my friend made several trips overseas to get things going. Nowadays with the internet, you more than likely wouldn't have to make trips to hook up with these products. The world has indeed become a much smaller place for all of us—and that is great news for corporate entrepreneurs.

FOREIGN LANGUAGE TRANSLATOR/ AIRLINE REPRESENTATIVE.

Yet another facet of sales representation is to seek out foreign airline companies, preferably in faraway places like Africa and the Far East. There are lots of immigrants living in enclaves in the US that save up their money for the specific purpose of going home to the "old country" from time to time. Take a place like Cambodia, there are large numbers of immigrants from that Southeast Asian nation living in tight-knit ethnic communities throughout the United States, yet many of the airlines serving that region have no sales representation set up. It perhaps doesn't make economic sense for them to retain one on a full-time basis, but they would no doubt be quite happy to have a representative calling on behalf of the travel agents and ethnic organizations. Remember, a round-trip ticket to a destination like Cambodia runs thousands of dollars, and often, these passengers travel in families and groups. It's the same for Africa and other remote (from the US) parts of the world. For many of the nations in such places, especially the smaller ones, the airlines have no full-time representation. Again, these airfares are big-ticket items and offer a marvelous opening for a sales rep to move in and fill the void. Make yourself their representative and reap the benefits!

It's all about thinking outside of the box, and in many cases, doing things or offering services for which there is a great need but others are not providing. If you're going to be a successful corporate entrepreneur, you have to constantly be thinking about what individuals and businesses need, and then figure out efficient and cost-effective ways of delivering it to them.

MALL KIOSK BUSINESS.

Expanding your horizons even further, another great potential business opportunity could be those ubiquitous kiosks that you always see at shopping malls these days. Sometimes you can contract with ten or fifteen malls at one time because they are run by one company, thus saving the time and effort of dealing with fifteen different people. These kiosks sell everything from sports memorabilia to sunglasses to cell phones and countless other items. They are relatively inexpensive to begin operation. You make an independent contractor agreement with the right individual (after a careful screening) and he or she then operates the kiosk, and you give them anything from 10 to 40 percent of the profits. As with many of these ventures, it would be impossible to overemphasize the importance of choosing wisely: the right person could quite literally make the difference between failure and success.

START A BLOG.

Another idea you may want to consider is starting a blog stemming from a personal passion, whatever that may be. Topics could range from politics, sports, music, and everything in between. Of course, there could be more specialized, unique things like antique collecting, historical memoirs, etc. One of the biggest topics online is relationships, so that is definitely something you may want to strongly consider for blogging.

Regardless of the subject matter, though, the basic premise is always the same: create a blog on the internet and get a lot of people interested. Then you sell internet advertising from your blog spot, perhaps even to major companies but essentially to any advertiser convinced that they would be a good fit for your audience. A friend of mine's daughter has a blog called *Our Freaking Budget*, and she makes a great income from it. They have all kinds of pop-ups and advertisements on that blog, so obviously this business model has been working out very well for her.

Keep in mind that, even though this is your own blog spot, and you can certainly write at least some of the content yourself, before long you will probably want to employ a couple of writers to help you keep the site up-to-date, useful, and interesting for your readers. Not only will this cut down considerably on the amount of time and effort you are going to have to put into the blog, but it's always a good idea to bring in new voices. These writers will interject a fresh perspective, which is of course something that your readers will dearly appreciate. They will start telling their friends about it. Word of mouth travels like wildfire in this era of the internet and social media. And in this business, more readers is the name of the game. When prospective advertisers see how popular a blog spot is becoming, their ad dollars are sure to soon follow.

I will now briefly take a look at other possibilities for your first business ventures beyond your day job. Please keep in mind that these are just snapshot descriptions. As we continue forward with this book, you will learn much more about the specific details of living as a corporate entrepreneur. For now, these are just a handful of suggestions to whet your creative appetite. There are countless other opportunities as well, limited only by the boundaries of your imagination.

CREATE A PODCAST.

A podcast is an audio message. It can be a radio-type

broadcast, a spoken political rant, a verbal journal, an instructional broadcast, an investment show, or a music program. It can be whatever you want to record and have your listeners hear. Of course, like anything creative, it has to be good, and here you're relying on your passion and talent in that particular area. You might spend an hour or two a day making each podcast. You would monetize the podcast through advertisers, just as with the blog spot concept, and hope to slowly grow your audience with creating something unique, sincere, and focused.

You would monetize the podcast through advertisers, just as with the blog spot concept.

CREATING AND DEVELOPING WEBSITES.

What's this all about? Well, it is one thing to have a nice, graphic, colorful website. But if you have no understanding or way of bringing customers to that website all you have is a pretty website. Companies (especially small businesses) have a strong need to design, develop, and promote their websites to the masses via search engines. This is a highly refined method of figuring out what words are most important when a person is searching for your product. It may seem obvious, like if you are selling accounting services so you use the word "accounting." That may or may not be. But more research could prove that another word is more effective and makes the difference between bringing in 'some' sales to bringing in 'a lot' of sales. This is called search engine optimization (SEO) and it's not as easy as it sounds, which is just one of the many reasons why a good website developer (and / or SEO specialist) is worth his or her weight in gold.

With this sideline, you can make money either on a flat fee or a percentage of sales, depending on what's most lucrative. In cases where it is a sales website, you can get a piece of that income.

Initially at least, one of the most challenging aspects of this type of venture is to get the gig in the first place and hiring the right kind of assistance that you might need. Once you're up and running, however, website development often leads to further opportunities, because as you're helping companies with their own online presence, you learn more about other companies out there and find more avenues of business that you can develop for yourself.

BECOME AN ADVERTISING CONSULTANT FOR SOCIAL MEDIA WEBSITES AND COMPANIES.

This can include but is not limited to offering strategy, asset development, lead generation, customer retention, and sales force optimization. I don't have firsthand knowledge of this type of business, but one of my friends has done it and has found much success with it. Start doing some research on this idea, and I think you will find that it fits in nicely with the corporate entrepreneur model, as it can be done remotely and does not require constant, round-the-clock attention. Social media is a growing phenomenon that shows no signs of slowing down, so there should be numerous opportunities in this field for years to come, and those who position themselves to ride the wave will be well rewarded for their foresight.

OFFER YOUR SERVICES AS A PERSONAL LIFE COACH.

This is where you set up a service to help others find more success in their life and in their career. You can do it on weeknights, late afternoons, and weekends and charge perhaps a hundred an hour. Therefore, even just five clients would make for a great sideline.

Ask yourself what kind of qualities are required for a life coach. First of all, you need to be *certain* that you have the ability and wherewithal to help others. In my life, I'm the go-to person on challenges. I can help others focus on the important things. Is the same true for you? Let's see. Ask yourself these questions. Can I help people through a crisis? Do I like sharing ideas? Can I help others to de-stress? Do I genuinely like people? If you have any or some of these qualities, chances are you have what it takes to become a life coach. You would also direct them to other areas of business that would be beneficial for them.

It is necessary to be certified or to get certified to become a life coach, but you can attain that through any of the numerous life coach certification outfits online.

The longer you work in this capacity, you get a better hold on it and accumulate even more knowledge of what's out there in the marketplace so that you can speak with great authority to your clients. I've probably coached twenty-five people within the last five years. I've been a guest on the radio to describe my experiences. We look at where our clients have been, what they want to do in life, and then find out what's holding them back.

There are so many people that have no direction and have been spinning their wheels for far too long. By helping to motivate them and guide their career in the right direction, you will at the same time be helping yourself as you use personal coaching as just one more additional way to enhance your extracurricular activities as a corporate entrepreneur.

CHAPTER 3

Choosing and Motivating Managers

SELECTING A MANAGER to run one of your businesses is always a crucial, if not critical, decision. It's one that can either make or break a business, especially when you as the owner are in a remote location. For the most part, success or failure will depend on this person whom you select. Remember, to a large extent this person is going to be virtually on his (or her) own. Of course, he will be talking to the boss (you) during the work week and he can expect a visit perhaps four or five times a year, but for all intents and purposes he's on his own. Yes, his progress can be noted and charted and he will be retained on the basis of performance and capability, with which his salary will be commensurate. That may seem simple and obvious, but if the person isn't doing well, a lot of damage can be done by the time you discover it to stop the bleeding. Stay on top of things. While it is certainly true that as a corporate entrepreneur you need to learn to delegate, that is no excuse to *abdicate* your role and responsibility as the owner of the business.

But there is much more to it than just whether the manager you choose is qualified. Some qualified people lack the proper motivation—at least the motivation that goes beyond earning a paycheck. Ideally, you want a person who in his gut feels that your business is in a very special way 'his own baby,' and it is not only a matter of money, but a matter of pride as to whether it's successful. Does this individual have what it takes to operate your business as if it were his own? That is the key question to keep in mind.

It goes without saying that the person should be experienced in the business. For example, in my health club business, I of course need someone who understands the fitness industry. Yet, managerial experience is not necessarily a prerequisite. There are lots of ambitious go-getters out there with a solid understanding of what makes a good health club tick. It could be a personal trainer or someone else at another level. In many cases, it's simply a matter of being in the right place at the right time. Maybe you can provide an opportunity with your new venture that someone was looking for but unable to attain at their present place of employment.

Regarding salary, if you were an onsite owner, you might be able to 'Scrooge' a little when it comes to compensation, but not as an entrepreneurial owner. You simply can't afford to be cheap and have to expect to pay at the top of the line level. A new manager can't go into the position with any doubts or reservations about things like an inadequate starting salary with a promise of more if he performs well. That would most assuredly start things off on the wrong foot for the ambitious twenty or thirty-something-year-old whom you hope to craft into becoming an integral part of your business.

If you bought an existing business or a franchise that already has existing employees, things are a little different.

When you're acquiring a franchise, in most cases it makes sense to keep the same manager. Still, be sure to do your homework and look into the situation so you can feel confident that a management change is not required. If it is, go ahead and do so. It is your business now, and one of the perks of ownership is the freedom to make the kinds of high-level decisions that only an owner can make.

When deciding on a manager, I think it is imperative for you to first interview the employees who are already working there. Then you will need to either hire from within or look to outside sources such as Craigslist to try to find the right individual. Let's say you have bought a franchise that is in pretty much virgin territory for that particular brand. It's either never been in that area, or you have the first franchise in that territory. Your first step for this new business is hiring, which includes the general and the assistant manager, ideally people who have done this job for a competitor. Since it's important to do the interviews in person, you will most likely want to arrange for them to take place on your vacation time or on weekends. Or you could have a close friend do it, but it has to be someone whom you really trust and have the utmost confidence in, because as mentioned, this selection is one of the most important factors in the business, at least initially. Also, with the explosion of Zoom meetings, you could now do these interviews yourself while at work on your lunch break or from the comfort of your own home! If you spend too much time "managing" the business yourself remotely, you will quickly see diminishing returns. That is unacceptable, but it should not and will not happen if you choose the right manager. So, choose wisely! If you have a lousy manager, his constant crises are to disrupt everything you are involved in at your primary job, as you will constantly find yourself putting out one brush fire after another. That is a huge no-no for any aspiring corporate entrepreneur, as you will be distracted by the problem business and therefore unable to concentrate on either your day job or other business enterprises.

SELECTION PROCESS

When you are hiring a manager, it all begins with the interview process. I like to have a full list of candidates, at least fifteen, from which to choose. One way to get these candidates is through the agencies available in the area where your business is located. So if I'm establishing a new business in South Dakota, I'm going to have them put the word out about the job opening in that region of the state.

I always need to first see a resume, and I also like a lot of follow-up phone calls. When I interview, I like to know how the candidate would behave in various situations, and my questions are geared toward eliciting realistic replies. How they handled this or that situation in their previous job is important too. I also need to know what tasks they undertook to make themselves or the company successful. Then I want to see if the person is an action person. I prefer a high-energy individual. If I tell them today that we have to do something for next week, I have to see that it is done expeditiously and without grumbling or mistakes.

There are always certain red flags that I keep an eye out for. One of them is when somebody is leery about giving me references—or when I do contact the reference, it is weak.

If I'm impressed with the candidate and they make it to the second interview, I might ask them for an example of a small business plan they would do for the business. If they come back with a real blockbuster plan with a lot of good stuff, that's a huge factor in his or her favor. I also like somebody who stays in contact with me. If they follow up, that is also a major positive. Every business owner needs a manager who knows how to exercise initiative.

A TV ad that satirizes this point is one where the interviewer, after saying goodbye, gets a phone call. It's the interviewee still sitting in front of him. The interviewee says, "I just like to follow up. How did the interview go?"

Besides a good belly laugh, this is what I'm looking for: eagerness!

Once you've hired a manager, how do you keep this person highly motivated? First, especially from the corporate entrepreneur point of view, you're going to have to let them make decisions on advertising, hiring, staff coverage, and all other routine matters for running the business. They are going to have to hire the team that will ultimately comprise the company's work force. Every sixty to ninety days, you're going to have to review the employees.

When it comes to the inevitable question of salary, it's always a good idea to tie compensation to performance for your manager, and you should develop different types of bonuses. Some will be performance-based, and some will be employee retention. Basically, you're going to give them a percent of the profits. The best thing to do is to pay bonuses twice a year. Quarterlies could change and be too soon to judge performance. You're better off biannually. You need a lot of confidence in the manager. It may seem obvious, but I can't stress enough that having a capable manager has to be the absolute first consideration if you plan on successfully running a side business, far away, while still keeping your day job.

You always want to be able to maintain frequent and steady contact with your managers, but you also want to make sure that they know that they are the boss. Yes, ultimately you are—but when it comes to day-to-day activities, the manager is the head honcho. You have to learn how to control your own ego. Just because you may be the boss and you're making seven figures, you don't need to outshine your managers. You need to be comfortable wearing two hats.

One advantage of keeping your day job is that you will likely run into other businesses with which you might want to become involved, or people who want to invest with you. Not only are you being paid by the entrepreneurial business, you continue to reap the benefits of having a full-time job.

Being a corporate entrepreneur is a category all its own. It is for a person who is skillful enough to learn how to enjoy the position of ownership from afar. For example, you may like to work out, but that doesn't mean you need to work out every single day, become a fitness guru, or anything like that. In other words, to be a corporate entrepreneur is to be a leader, and while a general may love to command, that doesn't mean he needs to be down in the trenches with the troops.

Once you have the right managers in place, you will be more freed up to concentrate your energy on other endeavors—for example, getting your day job clients to invest into one of your side businesses. While this may at first glance seem a bit risky, if done correctly with the right people, it can be a very good thing. Walking that tightrope is part of the risk-taker adrenaline rush you get as a corporate entrepreneur—and you should be able to walk it without falling off. Exercise extreme caution with whom you trust. I don't mean that you need to be paranoid—just prudent, and follow your instincts and best judgment when it comes to all business matters. Always do all of your due diligence, of course, but never fail to also listen to that little voice inside that keeps whispering advice to you. That is what probably got you interested in business in the first place, and it is highly unlikely that it will ever let you down.

CHAPTER 4

Your CPA, Your Lawyer, and Your Personal Assistant

THIS CHAPTER IS about choosing the three most important members of your corporate team. They are your CPA, your attorney, and your personal assistant. You need all three if you hope to find true and lasting success as a corporate entrepreneur. Think of these people as an investment in your own future—they will not only make life a lot easier for you, but utilizing their skills and talents will also help your businesses to flourish in new and unexpected ways.

A certified public accountant (CPA) is indispensable for a number of reasons. This is the talented individual who is going to prepare all of the financial records for your businesses, including federal and state tax filings. Getting your taxes messed up is one of the easiest ways to throw a fledgling business off track. You need a skilled professional with the knowledge and experience to handle all of the required filings accurately and on time. The IRS and your state's taxing authority are not very forgiving when it comes to mistakes. The penalties for inaccurate or incomplete returns can be quite hefty, so these are definitely not the kinds of issues you want to try to tackle yourself. They can also be tremendously time-consuming, so this wouldn't be a particularly wise use of your valuable time, either. Save the "do it yourself " stuff for fixer up projects around the house.

When trying to decide on the right CPA, a corporate entrepreneur should keep in mind the "60 percent rule." What is that? Simply put, it means that at least 60 percent of the prospective CPA's clients should be small business clients. You don't want to use the old bookkeeper type. That is someone who simply keeps the books and enters in all your sales, assets, and liabilities. That in and of itself is a really necessary job, but the fact of the matter is it does not rise to the professional level of the CPA. For these reasons and many others, I strongly advise that you obtain the services of a highly qualified CPA.

Never try to cut corners when it comes to hiring the right CPA, because he or she will become a part of your team who will be crucial for your success. In fact, the CPA needs to be one of the most professional members of your team. This person will, amongst many other duties, help to enable you to utilize the financial resources of banks and other financial institutions. For example, the CPA will produce such documents as profit and loss statements. These show your profitability or your loss (lack of profitability) during the fiscal year. Then there are balance sheets—these are an analysis of your assets and liabilities. Balance sheets ultimately show your net worth or lack of the same. Moreover, your CPA will be doing the taxes on your corporate returns. They need to know the federal tax code inside and out and be sure to take every legitimate deduction. When you get a refund, you are able to plow it back into the business and continue to grow it. To that monumental responsibility, add payroll records and a myriad

YOUR CPA, YOUR LAWYER, AND YOUR PERSONAL ASSISTANT

of other critical financial data, and you can readily see the value of bringing the right CPA on board.

Now I know some of you are probably asking, "But if I'm a corporate entrepreneur, that almost by definition means that I should be on top of financial things, so why pay the extra expense of a CPA?" While such a question may at first seem perfectly logical, upon closer examination you come to see the folly of it. Yes, you should indeed have a working knowledge of all of these issues, and you must definitely be well aware of the financial condition and circumstances of all your side businesses all of the time. However, there are very sound reasons why you're not going to get involved in producing any of these documents, and chief amongst these (in addition to the drain on your time) are education and experience. CPAs are highly trained professionals who have spent a lot of time in school learning their trade, followed by years of practical experience assisting other business owners just like you. When it comes to financial matters, they have seen it all and done it all.

You need to have answers when banks (or the IRS!) question your business! An important factor when you are interviewing and deciding on hiring anyone, including a CPA, is how quickly he or she returns your calls. Ideally you should receive a return phone call or email in a couple of hours. This not only tells you a lot about the individual's character and work ethic, it gives you an inkling of what to expect from them after they start working for you. For example, when a banker needs something and you contact your CPA, you will expect him to respond within forty-eight hours. A delay could mean missing out on a great opportunity and would of course be completely unacceptable.

The second key member of your team is your attorney. Nobody likes to get embroiled in legal conflicts, but as a practical matter, if you are going to delve into being a corporate entrepreneur, you can never expect to avoid them entirely. Think about it this way: in many cases, a good lawyer can be all that stands between defeat and victory in your business battles. I have had my share of them over the years, and I've come out on top almost every time— not only because I was doing things the right way but also because my attorney knows how to do his job properly.

The attorney should be a business-based lawyer who has some experience in litigation. They should have a large percentage of business clients. I usually recommend that at least 75 percent of their clients need to be businesspeople.

You should interview three or four prospective attorneys that fit that profile. He or she needs to be thoroughly experienced in business filings and organizations. The rule of thumb with a lawyer, perhaps even more than with your CPA, is that he gets back to you within the next day after you contact him with a need for services. If not, then you should probably find a new attorney.

There is no need to keep an attorney on a retainer; simply compensate them for whatever they do for you. Also, keep in mind (and this is especially true if you are worried about getting involved in legalities) that most times none of the disputes will actually wind up in court. On the other hand, you can't be worried or intimidated about being involved with the law. It's just a routine part of doing business. You need to stand up for yourself. Yes, you most certainly need a healthy dose of chutzpah to be a successful corporate entrepreneur.

As you diversify your businesses, you're going to need attorneys who are proficient in various areas—for example a real estate attorney, a tax attorney, or a litigation attorney. In a lot of instances, there will be insurance-related issues.

YOUR CPA, YOUR LAWYER, AND YOUR PERSONAL ASSISTANT

Last, but certainly not least, as a corporate entrepreneur, you will soon find that a personal assistant is indispensable. Hiring such a person is in fact imperative, especially once you have three or four businesses up and running. Your personal assistant will be able to organize and file all the "everyday" routine matters that you simply won't have the time to take care of yourself. Always keep in mind that you still have your day job to maintain.

Your personal assistant must be quite versatile, with the ability to understand and lend a helping hand for all of your various business enterprises. These days, almost every business usually requires a lot of reports and filings. Some of these are duplicative. Other than tax-related issues (which your CPA or attorney will handle) your personal assistant can be invaluable when it comes to keeping up with this seemingly unending flow of paperwork. The same is true for expense accounts and other mundane tasks, such as keeping track of receipts. Over the years, I've found that to be amongst the most monotonous and time-consuming tasks. I've had an assistant for fifteen years, and that takes the burden off of me. A guiding maxim in business is "time is money." So you need to look at hiring a personal assistant as, in reality, making a very wise investment not only in your business but also in your own future as a corporate entrepreneur.

The more you expand your enterprises, the more you will need a personal assistant. If you train them right, they will be interested in your enterprises. Therefore, in the long run, if this person does a great job for you, he or she might wind up taking a greater role, like an assistant manager, in one of your companies.

Learn from my personal experience; before I had a personal assistant, my day job performance lagged. As I mentioned, keeping track of receipts and filling out my expense accounts was a real drag. That's the sort of thing that drains your motivation and makes you lose your enthusiasm. Staying focused on your larger goals is why it's so important to have a person whom you deeply trust to take care of all of the small stuff for you.

It is probably best if your personal assistant can work in one of your offices. In my case, they were in the office of the storage company, meaning my wife and I had direct access. Of course, that's not always going to be possible, but it's ideal if you can make it happen and quite convenient for all involved.

As for work hours, ideally, thirty-six hours a week is fine. I've recruited personal assistants from Craigslist and other lists on which I advertise. Neighborhood websites are also very helpful in this regard. That's how I got my last personal assistant.

During the interview, you will learn whether the candidate has the requisite understanding and knowledge of what you will need them to do. They should, at the very least, have experience with fundamental tasks such as dealing with expense accounts, P and L's, and other necessary filings. Having worked as a personal assistant previously would, of course, be a major plus too.

Rather than hire this person as an employee, it's best to sign them up as a 1099, someone who is an independent contractor and takes care of his own taxes. Around $12.50–$20 per hour is a good wage, though of course there is a lot of flexibility. You should also work in some motivation for an increase in their compensation. What is most important, as with all three of these vital team members, is to find the right individual who is a perfect fit for both you, and for the businesses in which they will participate.

CHAPTER 5

The CEO in the Mirror

A CORPORATE ENTREPRENEUR is chief executive officer of all his or her business holdings—yet in very different ways from our standard perception of a CEO. One of the many advantages is that you have much more flexibility, since you own the businesses entirely. Even if you bring people in to invest in your business, so long as you maintain majority control, you will be the one with the authority to make all the important decisions. With the typical corporate CEO, he or she has lots of different people to answer to, from the board of directors down to the stockholders to whom he is obligated by a fiduciary relationship.

Nonetheless, despite all the independence and flexibility, as a corporate entrepreneur you will indeed shoulder a great deal of responsibility. First and foremost, success or failure will in large measure depend on how you navigate the often-treacherous waters of the business world on a daily basis. It will be up to you to develop and promote a strong leadership culture within all of the companies that you own and operate. This culture starts with you and flows down to your managers and assistant managers, and ideally should include everyone in the organization, even the part-time employees.

What is the culture of leadership? Though it can mean different things at different companies, it is basically an environment where everybody tries to do the absolute best job they can, and they are dedicated to the organization's success. It involves taking pride in the accomplishments of the business and understanding the value of being a team player. This is not optional! You cannot force your employees to participate in this culture, but you need to strongly encourage it. From top to bottom, everyone has to bring their "A" game; every day. The old cliché is very true and quite profound when you really think about it: any chain is only as strong as its weakest link.

It all starts with the hiring process. Take your time and be selective. Carefully go over fifteen to twenty resumes, thoroughly check out the references, and then be meticulous when it comes to interviewing. If you ask the right questions, the answers will help you tremendously when it comes to making your decision. The best person for the job will be the kind of individual who is truly driven to succeed and who understands and values the concepts behind the leadership culture that you are building. Most importantly, they should eagerly want to become an active participant in that culture.

For example, in the health club business that I operate, I have a discussion with my manager every single morning. We talk about how many potential clients we are going to try to close, and what kind of memberships we are going to sell. We also discuss, in quite a bit of detail, whatever promotions we are running.

After I have finished speaking with the manager, he (or she) then has a talk with the assistants and other members of the staff. It is critical that everyone remain on the same page.

Many of these conversations revolve around our use of guerilla marketing tactics. Whereas conventional marketing uses all the tried and true "old school" advertising methods like newspapers, TV, point of purchase, billboards, etc., guerilla marketing entails going unconventional. It is using low-cost, highly creative methods that catch the customer by surprise and leave an indelible impression on them by creating a lot of social buzz. It tends to hit them at a more personal and memorable level. It can be anything from distributing flyers publicly, to creating an operation at a major event without being directly connected to the event. In other words, it involves being creative and thinking outside the box. I try to encourage this mentality in everyone who works for me.

Our advertising campaigns have a different theme every ninety days. During that time period, we talk about our strategy. As a corporate entrepreneur, never make the mistake of thinking you have to be "the brains" behind every innovation in your business just because you are the CEO. If your managers and assistant managers have a fair amount of business acumen (which they assuredly will if you've hired the right people), they certainly are capable of new ideas too.

However, even if you don't personally develop the overall strategy, and instead do so in conjunction with the help of your team or teams (which I strongly recommend); at the very least you do need to be the impetus for the development of the strategy. You have to work the ninety-day plans. This means that you do everything possible to close the targeted number of sales in that timeframe. You even have your part-timers help you to bring in new customers (with health clubs, it's new members). This approach also works in any other business as well. How important is it to remain as inclusive as possible, and to keep these lines of communication open? One word: indispensable. I schedule conference calls once a week, but speak with the manager, at least briefly, every day. This requires setting specific time for phone calls. Often, I'll make those calls while I'm driving. What a great use of available time, that might otherwise be wasted! You may want to consider making the phone call a different time each day. This provides a hidden benefit; the people you manage never know when they are going to hear from you. If you call at a set time once and only once in any given time period, when they are done with your call they know they don't have to worry about hearing from you till the next call. In other words, the pressure is off them. You never want that.

This isn't about playing some sort of mind games with your employees. Yet, you do want them on their toes and thinking about success all the time. Ultimately, this is for their benefit, and in their best interests—as well as, of course, your own. Any strategy that leads to and promotes success benefits everyone involved. After all, if the business fails, they will be out of a job and you could lose a lot of money. A diligent, wise corporate entrepreneur who always keeps his or her finger on the pulse of the business will not let that happen.

For these reasons and many others, your focus on details must be as precise and intense as a laser beam. Do not confuse this attention to detail, however, with thinking that you must, in a hands-on way, address every detail. That would, first of all, be impossible. No matter how well organized, no one person could ever find enough time to personally take care of everything. Secondly, while you have the final and definitive last say on things, in your role as CEO, it is essential that you empower your managers to be able to make quick, strong decisions. Not only is that pretty much what you are paying them to do anyway; but equally important, it sends a strong message to them that you trust their judgment and decision-making ability. This will in turn bolster their confidence and make them better at their job.

The most successful leaders have mastered the art of delegating duties and responsibilities. This is true for presidents, to powerful corporate leaders of multinational conglomerates, and you will find, that it is extremely helpful for you too. Taking all that weight off of your shoulders, while nonetheless remaining in control of all your business holdings, is how you want to have things set up. Do it the right way, and the results could literally be life-changing.

Staying with the health club example, we have a regional manager and three assistant managers. I give them a great deal of autonomy. For instance, they are on their own when it comes to hiring. However, I like to be involved in the firing of individuals. No, it's not because I enjoy firing people! In fact, it's quite unpleasant, and I wish that I could avoid it; but I can't! It's part of doing business, and (sad but true) it can have an even bigger impact than hiring people. That's because when you fire someone, you run the risk of them coming back at you and claiming they have been treated unfairly. Lawsuit, anyone?

You always have to be very cognizant of a potential lawsuit. We've had it happen to us before, but we always take the proper course. I'm talking about creating a substantial paper trail. My policy is that an employee has to be written up three times before you fire them so that you can prove you have good cause. It is critical to always create and maintain the proper documentation. The best possible outcome when an employee is a bad fit is for that individual to simply quit. A voluntary termination of employment is so much easier to handle. Whatever you do, whenever it comes to this touchy issue, use a good deal of caution.

Let me also add that as CEO, you need to be sure to provide your company with all the proper resources that it will need to thrive. Competition is fierce, and it's easy to fall behind, and hard to always be playing catch up.

One of the most important things you can do to seize a competitive advantage is to not limit the resources you pour into your business. The best financial investment that you can ever make is allocating the money that you earn back into your own enterprises. That way, rather than stagnating, they will continue to grow. Like living organisms, just sitting still is never good enough in business. Learn from the most successful companies, both in your chosen fields, and any other fields as well. What do you notice? They are always innovating, always trying out new things, always growing. Emulate and adapt that mindset, and soon, you too, will enjoy that very same kind of success. Your most valuable resources, of course, are the people that you hire to run and operate your businesses; treat them accordingly. For example, we recently conducted a 'capabilities' review of our assistant managers and we're going to tie them into a potential performance bonus once or twice a year. This is necessary so that they have a stake in the game. We'll set the goals and make them aware of the potential rewards they will receive if they reach—or better yet, exceed—those goals. You will be amazed by how motivational that can be for them!

If one of my managers has a great idea to run by me, I will more than likely give them a chance to do it. A lot of businesses utilize trade shows and fairs that the lower-level people can be involved in, and although they can be a bit expensive, I've found them to be well worth it. Never underestimate the value of a participatory mindset when it comes to the folks who work for you.

Finally, always remember that as CEO, you need to be able to switch roles on a dime. That often means getting off one phone call and jumping right into another one—from another side business—and then smoothly transitioning right back into your day job. Obviously, that can be a challenge, no problem! Corporate entrepreneurs love challenges! How do you keep up with it all, without losing your mind? There are many techniques. One of my favorites is positive imaging. Think about how successful your businesses will be. Imagine the kind of money you are going to be able to make. Open wide your mind's eye and envision all the fun and exciting trips you will want to take...and then start planning for them.

The list goes on and on. We've talked about what motivates managers and employees. Well, in much the same way, all these positive images, which are as vast and as infinite as your imagination, are what motivates the most successful CEOs. Stay determined to join the winners!

CHAPTER 6

Knowing Your Limitations

AS A CORPORATE entrepreneur, you, of course, want to set your sights high and always believe that the sky's the limit. However, being a no-nonsense, "bottom line" businessperson, you also need to know your limitations. From a practical standpoint, just how many businesses can you own and operate? The answer to this question is crucial. It will vary from one individual to the next, but you have to analyze your circumstances, both personal and financial, before making any decisions that you may regret a bit further down the road. The purpose of this chapter is not to discourage you, but to make sure that you always approach each new venture through realistic eyes.

Not surprisingly, in approaching this topic we return to the basics. And when it comes to juggling multiple business operations, it all begins with how well we go about choosing managers. The manager's ability will in large part, either make or break each business. It also plays a huge role in how many side ventures you will be able to get involved with, while you are holding down, and continuing to thrive at your day job at the same time.

In my career, I have found that five businesses at one time is quite doable. But also consider, as I have in each instance, how does your spouse or significant other feel about it? Talk to him or her about the commitment of time and resources you will be making as you expand your business enterprises. What is their reaction? Gauge it discerningly. Be frank and brutally honest in your discussions about this topic. It is no doubt going to mean an increased investment of your time. Will that be okay? In what ways will your spouse or significant other be involved in this new venture, and what does he or she think of its merit? Though you often need to rely on your own gut instincts, for (quite literally) life-changing decisions such as these, everyone in your "inner circle" must be involved in this very deliberative process. Yes, most of it will be your own thinking, and you will be the final decision-maker on these matters. But the point that I want to emphasize here, is that when it comes to the question of Entrepreneurship--you don't (and probably wouldn't want) to operate as a "lone wolf." You need to have a support network in place that you can rely on for advice and guidance when it comes to taking big steps like this, that will have such a profound and lasting impact on your future success.

Having said that, if you ultimately determine that you are indeed ready for expansion, you have to tackle the question of where you are going to make your next move. One approach is to begin with a process of elimination. Let's face it; you're really not going to want to add a business if you're not inclined to like the industry. Regardless of how much you attempt to rationalize the benefits of getting involved with something that is far outside of your comfort zone, you simply cannot fit a round peg in a square hole; no matter how hard you try! Indeed, it would be an exercise in futility, and a hindrance to your progress rather than a catalyst.

For example, if you're a guy whose interests are construction, woodworking, hunting, and raising hunting dogs, you're probably not going to find much satisfaction or enjoyment in running a fine arts studio—and it is so vital that you have at least some affinity for what you are doing. Now, I fully realize that there may be exceptions, and I certainly don't mean to stereotype or offend anyone. I'm simply saying, go into each new business fully cognizant of both your strengths and your weaknesses, seeking out the former while carefully avoiding the latter. Keep in mind, however, if it's an area that you personally are not all that interested in, but your spouse or significant other is drawn to, then that kind of business may yet be a good fit. Ideally, you are matching businesses with personalities and interests. Though it requires due diligence like everything else, exploring fields that intrigue you can be one of the most fun and exciting elements of the entire corporate entrepreneur experience.

Above all, never forget that with every one of your side businesses, you're still going to have to mind the store. That means, amongst many other things, that you to have to manage the managers. As the CEO, that's your primary function. They have to look to you for direction. You are the boss, and you hold the purse strings. And at the end of the day, you have the most to win and the most to lose.

Managing managers is a skill that you will eventually come to perfect, but only after a lot of practice, along with some trial and error. You're going to have to keep a certain schedule where you talk to your managers on the phone at least two to three times a week. You're going to be meeting with them face to face four or five times a year--even more so if your side business is close to your home. The only way that you are going to be able to sleep at night is by ensuring that you feel confident that they are doing their job and doing it

KNOWING YOUR LIMITATIONS

right. A periodic review of business documents such as profit and loss statements is a must. This is where the CPA provides you the quarterly financials, which will help you keep track of how you're doing. Frequent communication with your managers and key personnel will go a long way toward determining the success or failure of any business that you own.

Make sure to have in place clear guidelines for your managers regarding precisely what, and under what circumstances, they should or should not contact you. One method is to use money as a guideline as to when you should be consulted. I've always liked to set the bar at a thousand dollars for a problem where I should be consulted. If it's a broken refrigerator or some other repair that is necessary, I want to be notified and apprised of the situation; in other words, things over and above ordinary operating expenses. our managers also need to contact you if there is any kind of emergency or police involvement, for example, if there is a break-in or a robbery. When it comes to expansion and considering another business, you always need to be prepared for the added expenses that will occur. This may involve taking out a loan. Of course, even if you are self-funding, you are still going to be taking on more risk by adding another business to your roster. At this writing we are in the process of opening our second health club. Our goal is ultimate expansion to five clubs because we were so successful on number one after only a year. We chose the right location, the right manager, and the right brand.

This is all stuff that you need to do (and more), to grow the business correctly. You have to grow your mentality and willingness for risk taking. You can't stand still in the same category of risk-taking. You're going to have to get comfortable with the idea of increased investment, and therefore, at least slightly elevated risk. I am not in any way suggesting you make reckless forays into the unknown. By the same token, I don't want you to ever forget that the willingness and the ability to take on risk are the heart and soul of every successful entrepreneur.

The rather obvious rule of thumb is this: if you are successful in your first company, that is a good indication that it may be time to go for it--and reach for more! However, on the flip side of that same coin, if you get involved in a new venture and things seem to not be working out, at what point do you make the decision to abandon ship? That is never an easy decision, but it is one that you must make once you realize that the business can't be fixed, and the time has come to cut your losses and move on to greener pastures.

Then there is the issue of diversification. The fear of "putting all your eggs in one basket" should not be easily dismissed as merely some worn-out cliché that has outlived its usefulness. Think about it, if all your side businesses are in one industry, and that industry then suffers a dramatic downturn, you are locked in, and will suffer right along with it--maybe even become a casualty if the attrition is bad enough. Now that truly is something to worry about! For example, not too long ago, the video rental business was thriving. Owning one of these franchises, or even a mom-and-pop operation, seemed like a great investment opportunity. Remember when there used to be one of these ubiquitous neighborhood fixtures seemingly on every other corner? But then new technologies such as digital streaming swept in and swiftly and unexpectedly altered the way consumers accessed entertainment, quickly snuffing out what had been, until only recently, such a promising business model.

A similar example comes to us from the so-called "do it yourself " yogurt shops. Over the past few years, hundreds of these interesting little places have sprung up all over the country. Unfortunately, however, the initial strong enthusiasm for the industry has apparently been misplaced. The current estimate is that one of every three of these shops is going to close their doors within the next five years. Why? Too much competition. Too high an overhead for a monthly lease. Think what a disaster it could be for you if you own five of them! Even the Small Business Administration doesn't want to back loans for these businesses anymore. The lesson here is, if possible, branch out in a few different directions when it comes to choosing entrepreneurial businesses—diversify your business portfolio. Just as you should never put all your money into only one kind of stock, the same principles apply to the side businesses that you choose to operate; and always expect the unexpected!

Regardless of the mix of industries that you settle on, however, in all cases time management is crucial when it comes to juggling multiple businesses. Of course, it also depends on what types of business you are engaging in. Some practically run themselves, whereas others are more hands-on. If you have a great manager, then naturally, you won't need to be in touch as much. Where you need to spend time 'strategizing' is when the company is brand new and needs careful nurturing. When you get past twelve months and you're in the black, the amount of time you need to spend on the business should greatly decrease. Maybe a half-hour phone call with your manager three times a week, also going over P and L's, and checking the books. Just be careful to never get too "comfortable" with any of your business ventures. That can lead to complacency, which as a corporate entrepreneur is never a good place for you to be. It might sound corny, but I will say it anyway: stay hungry! Never be the type who is satisfied to simply rest on your laurels. Your attitude should be: There will always be new mountains to conquer, and I can't wait to wake up tomorrow morning and start climbing.

Nevertheless, some corporate entrepreneurs avoid new ventures that might require a significant investment of time--for example, becoming the owner of a sandwich shop concept such as Subway. The requirement of time for owning these kinds of franchises can be huge. These businesses are open 24-7 and need a lot of attention. If you're already operating other businesses along with your day job, all these new responsibilities may seem just too overwhelming. After all, there are only so many hours in a day.

However, don't hastily squander what might turn out to be an amazing opportunity for you. Instead, be very businesslike about the whole situation and carefully assess the pros and cons of such time intensive undertakings. The bottom line is, knowing yourself and your schedule, will it be worth the necessary sacrifices? Look, there is a risk/reward ratio for practically everything that we do in life, and it is a very individualistic proposition. What might be doable and (in my mind) worth it for me, might be completely unacceptable for you. Neither one of us is "wrong" in our decision. In fact, we are both right, if the choice that we make is based on circumstances in our own life that would make this new business either a good or a bad fit for us. When you get right down to it, you know yourself better than anyone else in the world, which is why I believe deep introspection is the key when making the right decisions on big turning points in your career, such as this. So, trust yourself and your instincts.

KNOWING YOUR LIMITATIONS

Let me also mention here something that I briefly touched upon earlier—the idea of keeping a business journal. It can be very useful when it comes to making decisions. I have all my work documents hooked into my Excel spreadsheets. It helps me better manage my time and keeps me focused on what I need to think about the most on a day-to-day and month-to-month basis. In fact, a business journal is indispensable because it keeps all of this data highly organized. It has allowed me to identify certain areas where I've spent too much time with this or that aspect of one of my businesses where I didn't need to—for example, where the manager was fully capable of keeping everything operating smoothly. You can imagine how helpful that will be when it comes to making important decisions.

CHAPTER 7

Paying the Price

AS I'M SURE you can now see, becoming a corporate entrepreneur can be a very lucrative and rewarding avocation—but please keep in mind that it doesn't come without a price. I'm not talking about money! No, even more important than financial concerns, you must prepare both your body and your mind to cope with the rigors that accompany the new and sometimes daunting challenges you will inevitably face. That is why it is so crucial for you to develop a workable strategy for keeping yourself from burning out.

It would be impossible for me to overstate the value of relaxation when it comes to maintaining your peace of mind. I am not only talking about taking vacations. That almost goes without saying. But there are also countless other ways, besides your vacation, to relax. It is not something that you do just a few times a year when you feel worn out. To the contrary, you should develop a daily routine of relaxation that fits into your schedule. No matter how busy you are, find the time to make this happen! Trust me, you won't regret it. Of course, there are some methods that are going to fit you better than others, and we will discuss some of them. The point, however, is that all of us need at least a half hour to an hour of "down time" to clear our head each day.

The ideas that I will review in this chapter are not by any means the limit of what you can do to relax. In fact, there is no limit, as there will be as many different approaches as there are different human beings pursuing careers as corporate entrepreneurs. But I will list some of the most popular along with certain things that work for me personally.

Meditation is one method that offers a great way to relax. Like everything else, it may or may not work for you, but I would urge you to at least consider it. Daily meditation can alter your brain's neural pathways, thus resisting, or at least reducing the severity of stress. What exactly is meditation? While the precise definition can vary from one individual to the next, it doesn't have to be anything complex, and it certainly doesn't require any sort of special training or instruction. In fact, it can be as simple as sitting quietly and alone for fifteen minutes closing your eyes, perhaps repeating something soothing, like "I feel peaceful." Or just saying it mentally. The point is, you want to put your mind at ease, even in the middle of your most hectic day.

Then there are breathing exercises, another ideal way to relax. Again, you will want to close your eyes as you sit alone and in a quiet place. Draw in each breath slowly through your nostrils, hold it a moment, and then exhale through your mouth. Almost immediately you will feel your heart rate slow down. You will also feel your muscles begin to loosen up. Just don't become so relaxed that you fall asleep! (Yes, there are some experts who suggest taking "power naps" during your workday, but that is a whole different topic that we are not addressing here.)

Muscle relaxation can assume other forms, too. For example, sitting in a comfortable position, you can tighten your hand, hold it for ten seconds, and then release it. Do that with both of your hands and both of your feet. At the end of this exercise, you will feel the release of a lot of tension and a kind of natural peacefulness. I'm not suggesting some sort of deep spiritual experience or anything like that, but numerous studies have suggested that when you physically relax your muscles like this, you improve your overall general sense of well-being, both physically and mentally.

Another form of meditation is music therapy. This is when you relax by listening to the music of some of the greats—Mozart, Brahms, Beethoven, Schubert, to name but a handful. Being able to start the morning with a coffee or tea and listening to such music, works really well for me. Get in some (non-business) reading, too. That's another great way to start the morning that I really like. Not answering e-mails, phone messages, etc. There will always be time for replying to e-mail or returning phone calls later. Make sure that at least some portion of the day is reserved solely for "me" time. It's not being selfish. It's simply being healthy.

Other relaxation ideas (if it is something that you are into) might include getting on social media. Talk to friends. Update your Facebook "wall." Look at family pictures or other updates that friends or relatives have recently posted. You get the idea. Just take a much-needed break (temporarily, of course!), to forget about business and unwind.

Along these same lines, you should make it a habit to take daily breaks for tea or coffee and couple that with an exercise routine of some kind. It doesn't matter what type of exercise, anything at all that will get your blood flowing and unleash all of those "feel good" endorphins that the body produces when we exercise.

Speaking for myself personally, I do about thirty minutes of my own kind of meditation every day with barely any exceptions. Again, everybody will be different about this. For me, if I do thirty minutes of relaxation prior to a thirty-minute workout, including weight and cardio machines, I find I have a more productive session.

I vary my meditation schedule every day. Occasionally it will come first thing in the morning, but depending on my workday, I can sometimes do it at lunchtime.

As I said earlier, keep in mind that relaxing, while seemingly universal, is so personal and individualized that what may be relaxing for one person might be the total opposite for someone else. For example, some people might think a round of golf is relaxing. Other people, however, might find it an exercise in frustration. You know yourself better than anyone else will ever know you, so it's really just a matter of figuring out your own best strategy for relaxing, and then—most importantly—carving out time in your busy schedule to commit to it.

Another good example of relaxing is socializing with others. Maybe for you, that is one of your favorite forms of relaxation? I know, for a fact, that is true for many people. Of course, that can depend a lot on whom you are socializing with, as I know that (for me at least) some people leave me exhausted and worn out. Perhaps it's the same for you too?

The list of what is or is not relaxing is almost endless. Here are just a few ideas:

Some people think time in front of a TV screen is relaxing. (Of course, it probably depends entirely on the subject matter you are watching.) Some feel that time at the beach is relaxing (again, there will be lots of variables such as weather, traffic, crowds, etc.). Let's expand the possibilities a bit, because we're not just talking about daily relaxation. Periodic vacations are an absolute necessity too, especially when you consider how hectic the life of a corporate entrepreneur will always be, almost by definition.

Our rule of thumb is to take a three-day vacation at least every ninety days. If you can manage it, take even more time off than that, like a week or so or maybe a long weekend vacation. This is when I completely shut down. This is a time when I don't have my computer or iPad with me. I out and out relax. Some of the best relaxation spots are in Mexico, like Puerto Vallarta or Cancun, or the islands like Jamaica, or the Bahamas. Someplace where you really are *away* from it all for the entire time.

I have found that the "every ninety-day rule" to recharge the batteries works extremely well—Don't forget! You're working hard at both your daytime job and all your side businesses. If you don't take a break, you're heading for burnout. It will not be a matter of *if* it will happen. No, it will only be a matter of *when* it will happen—and how severe the physical and mental crash will be. You have to vigilantly guard against that. Mental health is as important as physical health, and vice versa.

You might also find it extremely relaxing to go camping either with a tent, trailer or an RV. This can be one of the most enjoyable, often understated, forms of relaxation. We know many people that use RVs to get away as often as possible. They do it in conjunction with their businesses, or their kids' activities, such as soccer, softball, and gymnastics. Here you're blending in camping and family activities. After all, there is only so much time in any given day, week, or month, so you need to be creative in how you spend it.

The bottom line is, don't neglect the things you enjoy doing because you're so caught up in business. That old cliché about avoiding being "all work and no play" is actually very wise advice.

Also, keep in mind that weekends can be immensely valuable for a corporate entrepreneur, both for completing tasks that you can't get to during weekdays and when it comes to relaxation. The best way to handle weekends is to work Saturdays; working at least half to three-quarters of the day will be necessary when you're involved with your entrepreneurial businesses. There's no way to get around working a little extra on your weekend off. However, Sunday (the traditional day of rest) is a good day to get away from everything. Maybe you attend religious services? Go out to your favorite restaurant? Watch sports all day? There is no "right" way when it comes to rest and relaxation. But there is definitely a "wrong" way, and that is bringing the worries and concerns of your business life crashing into time that you have set aside to get away from all of that. Don't allow this to happen! We stress how important it is to be disciplined when it comes to work. Well, the same applies to not working, too, especially if you're a real go-getter (which is a good thing, just be careful not to overdo it).

Assuming you have several weeks of vacation at your day job, how do you use that time as a corporate entrepreneur? It may vary somewhat from one enterprise to the next, but within reason, you should still be available for your businesses. If you're not available, you have to let your managers know ahead of time. That's why three or four-day trips are better than taking off for a whole week.

Vacations won't be all that relaxing if you don't ensure in advance that you will have peace of mind. Therefore, you need to go over things with your managers in a teleconference so that you can take some time off, and not spend it worrying about business-related issues! When you leave your teleconference, you should be rest assured knowing that things will be taken care of when you are away. You defeat the purpose of trying to relax, if you go away and are constantly thinking and worrying about your businesses. Be sure to go over every possible contingency with your managers before you leave town. And then just go ahead and enjoy yourself for a while! Not only is it crucial for your mental and physical health, but also, make no mistake about it, you work hard all year and deserve a break now and then--as does your family! Not to mention, if you are worn out and end up stressed to the max—and maybe even in the hospital—then you won't be of much use to anyone, either at your day job or at any of your side businesses. So be good to yourself.

To make sure that things work out the way you want, you need to be sure that you can focus on having some fun, rest, and relaxation without any interference from your business responsibilities. That's the most pleasant and efficient way to recharge those batteries every so often. And your family will thank you too!

CHAPTER 8

Distributorships

WE BRIEFLY MENTIONED distributorships in an earlier chapter as a possible pursuit for an ambitious corporate entrepreneur (okay, so *all* corporate entrepreneurs are ambitious, but you get my point). In this chapter, I'd like to show you in a little more detail just how to make this happen. At its most basic definition, working a distributorship usually involves assembling sales organizations for manufacturers, products, or services that don't currently have any direct marketing. either in your area, or perhaps, anywhere in the entire country. So you're primarily functioning as the middleman or marketing arm for a manufacturer or a service company. It could be a US-based company that's new and doesn't want to go through the expense of recruiting a sales force, or it could be an international company that does not yet have access to markets in the United States. Or they could simply feel that they don't have the expertise that a professional sales organization would have. Whatever the case, your job will be to sell their products within the United States.

Distributorships can be some of the most lucrative and important marketing arenas for marketing and sales personnel.

You can have the best product in the world, but if you don't have a good sales organization, you are not going anywhere! Your superior product will sit on the shelf while a good sales team will successfully sell an inferior product.

To be a truly successful distributor for a company or service, the individuals involved not only must have really good people skills, but they should also have solid experience with a good sales record. Does this sound like you? If so, you should seriously consider a distributorship as one of your sideline businesses.

I have partnered with a fellow sales professional for various distribution ventures. He and I have almost sixty years of combined sales experience between us. So it probably comes as no surprise that we were both aware that the first thing we needed to do was to identify a consumer need in the business world. Here again, working in familiar areas is helpful. In our case, with our Big Pharma backgrounds, we saw there was a lack of medical devices and specialty products in the med spa arena. We saw a gap and began investigating what products there were in the marketplace that might fill this gap. We looked for companies that had premier, very practical and cost-effective products but no marketing arm. We found them everywhere from New Jersey to Silicon Valley to overseas.

We began by contacting these companies and telling them we had groups of people ready to create a sales force. We advised them that we could set up anywhere from thirty-six to forty-eight month contracts to be their exclusive marketing arm for the US. We felt that with all our sales reps, we could handle three solid products. The first was a light therapy machine, and the manufacturer was based in Silicon Valley. Its primary function was to increase collagen supply in the face. This machine was spectacular, and ideal for med spas, because it helped to eliminate fine lines in the face. It was based on a light renewal system that used LED lights; it used red light therapy, blue light, and a combination of both red and blue. These frequencies tended to take care of wrinkles. It basically eliminated 'years' from the face. It also killed acne bacteria. This was most useful to those spas that dealt with patients that had acne and redness or flushing of the skin.

The second medical device was basically a large band that looked like an oversized blood pressure cuff. Primarily utilized to relieve pain in the arms, shoulders, and back, it also helped speed the healing process and stimulated the lymphatic system. Moreover, it promoted cell generation. We felt the two products were a good combination of overlapping technologies. The infrared therapy also helped relieve stress, eczema, and insomnia. We also sold this unit mostly to wound care clinics.

We also sold a Manuka honey type product through a company based in New Zealand. They made products like anti-wrinkle serum, first aid antiseptic lotion, anti-fungal cream, and anti-itch cream. We not only sold the honey but we found different types of products that utilized the honey.

The light therapy machine would sell for about fifteen thousand dollars. We discussed a deal with the manufacturer to be able to get them at a reduced rate and use them as our demo machines, and then we were able to couple these demos with all of the sales material.

We already knew we wanted to sell a product in the medical devices space. We narrowed it down to that device because we were not only able to do the light therapy machine with a US-based company, but it was something that was genuinely needed in medical spas. We then did our due diligence. Our prospective customers liked the idea because there was nothing like it on the market at that time. The medical spas could not only do well, but their patients would do well too, which was a huge consideration (you should always feel good about what you are doing to make a living!).

We make our initial approach and first contact by phone and email. We interview them and they interview us. It's kind of a little dance we do back and forth. After we've decided on the product, we ask them if we can come out and have a meeting with them at their office. This, of course, involves travel, but since personal contact is indispensable in sales, you will simply have to find a way to adjust your schedule accordingly.

My partner has always been great on the computer, which comes in very handy when it's time to make a first-class, knock-them-off-their-feet presentation. We would talk extensively about our plans for reaching the correct target market, and our sales goals. By now, of course, they would already be quite familiar with our extensive sales backgrounds and years of expertise. With the right combination of persistence and professionalism, we usually sewed up the deal on the second to fourth visit. Our contract would stipulate that we would be the exclusive distributor and spell out in explicit detail (after checking it out with our lawyer) all the terms, conditions, and obligations of both parties.

Also, we would discuss related issues such as the costs of promoting their products at international meetings and trade shows. That is why, before signing contracts, you should always first decide how and who will pay your expenses and fees. We did a tremendous volume of sales at trade shows. In my opinion, there could never be too many of them to attend.

The exclusivity built into the contract would be for a particular area, the geographic region that you are most capable of covering. But don't limit yourself unnecessarily. For example, when I was doing wrist watch distribution, we covered all of North America.

Let me point out that you don't have to stick to products you know something about or are interested in, although there is a definite advantage in that. On the other hand, your chances of success in something you know absolutely nothing about will be considerably lower.

We organized a sales network of thirty to fifty reps across the nation. We had a lot of connections from being in the pharma business and knew about 350 people nationwide. Some were working, some were retired, and some were in their own business and willing to be contractors. We had a list of 250 individuals on an Excel spreadsheet with all their contact information, who they worked for what their capabilities were—all the details of their resume. We updated this database every so often. We'd contact these people, especially when we had a potential breakthrough regarding new products. We found out whether they'd be able to rep them in their area.

Again, all this is from our personal background and experience. Yours, of course, would be no doubt, very different.

Our personal responsibilities included doing the trade shows as well as training the sales reps. We would be sure to have the machines available at our meetings so we could conduct training. We also provided our reps with all the sale literature, paraphernalia, and devices they might need to demonstrate and sell the products that we were representing. They would get everything they needed to sell effectively.

We'd sometimes go out with them about one day a week and help them sell. It was a vacation day or other personal time we could use away from our daytime jobs. Normally this would take place during the first ninety days of the product launch.

The commission for the rep was a straight 10 percent. Higher commissions would depend on how well they did sales wise. We'd have contests and times when we'd pay extra for exemplary performances. Many of these salespeople also went on to sell other products for us. They made a good living during our six years in business. They sold medical devices in med spas, and we also had devices that were actually sold in a whole different sphere of influence. These were machines that were sold to wound care centers. How were they able to do it, and at the same time make very good profits for my partner and me? Experience. There is simply no substitute for it in the world. These men and women were highly specialized reps who had already had illustrious careers in Big Pharma.

In our case, word never got back to my company about these activities. Some of our reps were working for the same companies we were working for. So in effect, they were corporate entrepreneurs working for corporate entrepreneurs. It was all very professional and everybody involved knew what was going on and how the game was played.

There are any number of distributorships you could get involved in. It could be wrist watches, it could be clothes, it could be high-end pens, and it could be all different types of jewelry. It could be just about anything. Let's say office equipment. You could set up something with Korean or Chinese office equipment companies (new ones are trying to enter the US marketplace all the time).

We've done inflatable toys, tents, and musical instruments. We also sold cigars, fine tobaccos, wines with no US distributor from Australia, computer parts, cars, and RVs. It's really too numerous to list.

The best advice is start out with something you know something about and then diversify. For example, even though this doesn't involve a distributorship, I have always had a passion for working out, but I never dreamed of owning a health club.

To sum up, stick to an area or products you have an interest in. Start off with something you know before branching out to different areas. At least in my own experience, that template has always served me well. And I'm willing to bet that the right distributorship can do the same for you, too.

CHAPTER 9

Minding the Store

WE'VE MENTIONED DUE diligence several times throughout this book. However, what is actually involved? Are there steps that the corporate entrepreneur needs to take that might not readily come to mind? It all depends on the circumstances. Sometimes opportunities get thrown in your lap. In other words, the business finds you. For example, we have a new health club that is going into the ideal demographic area, which among other things has a high population density. Now, the twist (i.e., opportunity) involves the business right next door. It is a women's clothing store that recently moved out. My wife and I, along with the club's general manager, realize that we have three plays here—we could instantly expand the health club and add a cross-fit area, we could put a new restaurant concept in the space, or we could just do nothing and let the landlord find a tenant.

Now comes the due diligence. The research involved in getting a new restaurant business up and going is super important because of the phenomenal failure rates of restaurants in general, let alone a new and pretty much untried concept. One of my best friends, John, is a restaurateur. He owns three different restaurant businesses in seventeen locations. A professional restaurant man, he knows everything from *A to Z*. So our health club general manager and I arranged three different teleconferences which John ran. The first teleconference involved the franchise headquarters people. The second and third involved actual franchisees. John was the one who gave the idea a thumbs-up or a thumbs-down. We trusted him because he always did a great job. He's the one who we listened to the most regarding this venture, and rightfully so. After all, you can't argue with success. His expertise also involved hiring and firing of personnel, but that's a whole new future topic.

The due diligence in this case was aided by the fact that we chose a nationally branded franchise. The franchise company was chock full of information regarding demographics, operations management, and what makes their top franchisees so successful.

The research on our part involved contacting these top franchisees to pick their brains and answer our questions about the franchise, such as the costs of labor, availability of labor, the brand acceptance in the area, and of course, the bottom line we might expect. An overriding question that we asked (in confidence of course) was: What did the franchisee really think about the home office?

Followed by: Were they as cooperative as they advertised? *Were they fair? Did they go the extra mile for one of their franchisees? Were they financially stable?* We realized that they didn't have to assist us with our business venture, but in a franchise organization there is a spirit of cooperation with other prospective franchisees.

This franchise is an interesting new concept with a unique name. There are only a few at this point and so it is important to learn whether the franchisee benefits as much as an old established franchise. We found that the downside was possibly the menu. This only made sense, of course, because they were mainly in the Southern states where Southern-style food was a bit more acceptable. High calories/high fat content seems to be a no-no for the Midwest.

Since our restaurant guy could speak "restaurant language," he was our point man. He's worth his weight in gold. He was leery about the menu for our potential location, and we backed out. We decided to expand the health club instead. Without his help during due diligence, we could have made a huge mistake.

For the most part, the research was the same as you would do with any other business. You would do it even if you were starting a place from scratch. What are they doing right? What are they doing wrong? What does the trade press say about them? Is confidence in them high or not? These are amongst the most crucial of the first steps in doing your due diligence.

Let's go back to the initial idea of starting any new business. Would you build a brick-and-mortar shop or would you start an internet business? Keep in mind that there will always be a need for brick-and-mortar businesses, and internet businesses typically have a much higher probability of failure.

The next step is where are you going to locate? You're better off getting involved with a real estate broker. You need a good one who knows the area and has a more than passing familiarity with the business community. About 99 percent of the time, the ones who are selling are paying the broker's fees. So it costs nothing to search within an area.

Commercial property is totally unlike residential. You don't have the peaks and valleys with commercial property that you do with residential since the very purpose of commercial property is fundamentally different from residential.

You have a choice of purchasing a place, building a new

one, or leasing one. As with anything, there are advantages and disadvantages to each. If you build, you are making a hefty investment in the whole business prospect of the area. If you are not successful, it could be difficult to sell a retail space that is specifically designed for one type of business. For example, a restaurant has its own unique setup and is divided between seating area, kitchen, and lobby. This might not be readily adaptable to, say, a retail outlet, which of course would drive the potential price down.

If you lease, you don't have any of these problems, but every time you renew the lease, you have to worry about the landlord jacking up your rent. Also, if you lease, you don't have the inherent value with real estate's usual tendency to *appreciate*. In the case of our new restaurant, however, the idea was to lease. There were a few reasons for this, but mainly because we wanted it to be close to our health club.

You must also look closely at the demographics of the area you are researching. You need to figure out the dollars to make sure that the business will be able to sustain the rent. It should be 10 or 15 percent of total sales. This is something that you should try to determine right away. Within a 30-50-mile radius, you need to get as much information as possible about their gross sales. If their sales don't meet the expectation, you would be foolish to move forward.

In addition to knowing the projected revenues, it's crucial to also understand who your potential customers are. Use common sense. You're not going to put in a skateboard park in the villages of Florida that cater to retirees. You need to know what percent of the targeted age group actually resides in the area.

A good approach is to spend a couple of days driving around the area and stopping in other, similar businesses and observing the customer flow. In short, you need to be located in an appropriate area. In our case, the specific demographic you would want for the restaurant would be between seventeen and sixty years old. It's a fairly low-price economy place, so it is important to have a somewhat young crowd available. Remaining cognizant of such factors is key.

Next, you must figure out how you are going to be able to pay for everything--How much bank or other financing will need to be involved--Whether you will do group financing, where everybody contributes a certain amount. Each different type of business, from restaurants to skating rinks, and everything in between, has a different threshold for financial stability. For example, right now the Small Business Administration (SBA) won't even finance a lot of restaurant concepts. Restaurants are considered high risk, which of course can be a turn-off for lenders, meaning you may have to invest your own capital into the venture, perhaps involving partners as well.

I know at this point some of you may be asking, "Well, what about performing due diligence regarding online companies? How does that differ from brick-and-mortar businesses?" One big difference is that with brick-and-mortar situations, the due diligence would be more accurate because a lot of it is dependent on the metrics related to actual existing businesses. When you are doing an online business, in most cases you are the one who is creating it, and there isn't much, if any, data about anything similar for you to make comparisons. That is why it is best to utilize online businesses as an extension of your "real world" enterprises.

Of course, there are exceptions. A good example would be the Casper Mattress Company. It is a firm that sells exclusively online. It is a combination of a Tempur-Pedic type mattress coupled with a latex interior. This mattress was tested, and it is known that a wide variety of people can sleep on it. They have been successful with their business model of keeping their operations purely online.

As I said, though, for most corporate entrepreneur situations, the online function is to enhance sales. In our watch distributor business, for example, we have an online site for the high-end watches. We sell direct to consumers. Moreover, all our health clubs are tied in to an online service where all the new customers are able to purchase memberships online. When we're doing group sales or grand openings or conducting a membership drive, they are all offered online. Online is an invaluable tool.

If you're purchasing a franchise, the HQ of that company will be able to assist you to enhance your current online marketing. Restaurants and numerous other businesses have become quite creative at this. They have come up with coupons, shout-outs, pop-ups and more. You have to have social media along with this too. Should you hire an IT person? Hopefully your general manager has enough knowledge about these things to save you that expense, which is something which you will learn in the interview. If they are in their late twenties, they will almost certainly have a firm understanding of the ins and outs of how the online environment operates.

The most important factor here is after you've done all the due diligence and research, you also have to do a constant self-assessment, a kind of self-awareness of your own abilities and of all your sideline businesses. How exactly this works largely depends on each kind of business. You're going to be poring over P and L statements and monthly revenue intakes for some, while for others, for example short-term rental properties, that won't be necessary because the fixed costs more or less remain constant. In our long-term rental homes, you just want the current residents to remain happy. You simply continue collecting the rents and keep the place up. With the storage complexes, it is the same kind of strategy.

For other businesses you'll have a constant moving target, especially the ones where you need to always get new customers. One of the things about new customers—the manager has to have a list of potential clients at all times. In that instance, you are assessing quarterly. Short-term rentals might require four assessments per year; in the health club business, you are doing a month-to-month assessment.

Do a day-to-day assessment on your day job, too. This is a perfect example of what I've been referring to as minding the store. You have to keep on top of every aspect. You need a plan that is going to maximize your performance. I use my smart phone--I know exactly where I'll be going every minute of every day. I have a daily plan. It is the only way that you can diligently mind the store and become truly successful as a corporate entrepreneur.

By the way, this should apply to the general managers of your side businesses as well. You need to find out what their day-to-day activities look like. I always ask them to do their own self-assessment every day. You can't ever do enough self-assessment. Ultimately, it is the best form of due diligence for every business that you own and for yourself.

CHAPTER 10

The Virtual World

IN THE PREVIOUS chapter, we briefly discussed online marketing. This topic has become so crucial for businesses that I want to explain more about it in greater detail. Think about it. What is the first thing that you would do today, as a consumer, if there were goods or services that you needed? You get on your laptop, tablet, or smart phone and start your research. That's simply how things are done in the twenty- first century. And even if you consider yourself a low-tech, "old school" kind of person, it is essential that your business ride the crest of the latest technological trends. This is where you will connect with your customers, and since your competitors are utilizing the online environment to their advantage, you literally can't afford to be left behind.

Although it is highly advisable that you hire outside help when it comes to online marketing, as we mentioned earlier, chances are your "IT person" could very well be the general manager that you've hired. Nonetheless, as a corporate entrepreneur, you never want to leave any facet of your side businesses (especially something as important as online marketing) completely up to other people, no matter how much you may trust them or how much confidence you have in their skills and know-how. You still want to educate yourself on how these things work. There will be strategic decisions to be made in many areas of online marketing, and if you don't have a clue as to how any of it works, how will you ever be sure if you are making cost-effective, intelligent decisions that will grow your business and maximize your profits?

I'm not suggesting that you become an expert in this area or take classes or anything like that. I am, however, going to show you the basics of how today's businesses (I'm mostly referring to brick-and-mortar establishments) are using the power of the internet to attract new customers and to keep in touch with and build up a rapport with existing customers.

Website Development

Once upon a time, company websites were simple—just one or two pages of basic information about the business and not much more. Surf online right now for even a few minutes, of course, and it's easy to see how much all of that has changed. Today, websites have lots of colorful graphics, videos, links to other websites, and a whole lot more. Trying to "do it yourself," unless you are extremely proficient with computers, would be a classic case of being penny-wise and pound-foolish. The money that you save will quickly be eaten up in missed customers and lost revenue because prospective customers were turned off by the bad first impression they received when they visited your amateurish-looking website.

I know that sounds unfair. Your company may offer far better products and services than any competitor does. But if your competitors all have top-notch, professionally designed websites, guess who is going to get the lion's share of the business? Like it or not, that is just the way consumers think today, not just the younger ones, either. Consumers of all ages and from all walks of life are either impressed—or not so impressed—with a business the minute they click on your website. I'm sure you've done the same thing yourself. We all do. If the website catches your eye right off the bat, then you start poking around the rest of the site and already you have become a possible customer. Conversely, if the site really turns you off because it looks like a fifth-grader designed it (no offense to fifth-graders; some of them really know their way around the web!) the web surfer is unlikely to ever make it past the website's home page.

Given all these considerations, spend the money to have your businesses' websites professionally designed and maintained. Not only will it save you the stress of attempting to do it yourself, but it will also give your business a first-class online appearance, that over the years will make you lots of money and enhance your reputation.

SEO

Okay, now that you've made the commitment to building a website that you can be proud of, you can just sit back and wait for all those online visitors to surf on over and see it, right? Wrong! How can they, if they don't know that it's there in the first place? In other words, locating your website on the vast internet can be like finding the proverbial needle in a haystack.

Fortunately, there are solutions for this seeming dilemma. One way is to "optimize" the site's "ranking" in the most popular internet search engines such as Google and Yahoo. Search engine optimization, or SEO, again requires the involvement of experts in this field (it may be the same person who designed your website, but probably not, unless they specialize in both). These folks know how to add into your website the right "keywords" and other features that will make the search engines list your site further toward the top of the page when users type in certain keywords or phrases. For example, type in "shoe stores" and see what comes up. You can further refine your search by also adding in the name of the town where you are looking for shoes. But why do some shoe stores' websites show up higher on the search results page than others? There can be many reasons, but one of the most critical is the content of their website. Much of this involves coded material deep in the background that human eyes never see. However, the complex algorithms of the website are well aware of these little gems, and a skilled SEO guy or gal knows just where and how to place them. Take advantage of their expertise and be one of the websites that prospective customers see first—and stop losing business to your competitors.

Pay Per Click

If you want to take things a step further, although it will cost you a little money, you may want to seriously consider utilizing "pay per click" advertising. This is where you create an advertisement for your business and then pay the search engine company (Google, Yahoo, etc.) a certain amount of money (you get to bid on the amount and set a daily budget) every time a searcher clicks on your ad. The ad will contain a link bringing the prospective customer to your website, and the search engines make all kinds of tools available to you so that you can keep track of how effective these advertising campaigns are for your various businesses. They let you know how many "conversions" or visits to your websites come from the various clicks that you receive each day, and that way you can adjust your daily budget or your advertising approach accordingly. This is a great way to get to (or near) the top of the search engine rankings, even if you are a fairly new business.

Social Media

These days, whether it's Facebook, Twitter, Instagram, or countless other platforms, people spend large portions of each day conversing on and perusing social media. This is great news for corporate entrepreneurs. Why? Because social media is an ideal medium to "spread the word" about your products or services. Establish an online social media presence (even if you have to hire someone to do it for you) and immediately you will be "connecting" with both new and existing customers. This creates a powerful psychological impact, as these people get to feel as if they know you and you, them. As you interact through these "friendly" platforms, those who have had a good experience with your business will then tell their friends about it. And they tell their friends about it. Before you know it, hundreds if not thousands of people who previously knew little or absolutely nothing about your business now want to become customers. Marketers of previous generations could only dream of such tremendous opportunities to be so easily accessible.

Professional groups and associations also have powerful online presences, and by joining these groups, amongst the member benefits, you can usually link your website with the organization's site. This not only draws in more traffic to your site, but it also shows the public that your business is successful and is run by serious professionals.

When it comes to using the internet for marketing, it's all about keeping your company's name in front of the public in every way possible. For example, take an automobile dealership. In the past, these businesses had no use for the internet. Today, they use it for everything from announcing sales, to giveaways, to showcasing their inventory, and to special promotions. Yes, they still use newspaper ads, radio, TV, and other "old media", but any dealership that neglects their online presence is surrendering a tremendous share of the potential customer base to their competitors. No business, in any industry, can ever afford to do that--least of all a hardworking corporate entrepreneur who wants and needs to take advantage of every opportunity presented themselves by the marvelous, day and age that we live in today.

The internet is your chance to draw in customers from far and wide, and depending on your product or service, your reach could expand from next door, to halfway around the world. Moreover, the internet is up and working day and night. How great is that? You can make money even while you're asleep! The key, of course, is to first put in the necessary work, and educate yourself while you are yet wide awake. Get started on this crucial aspect of your business enterprises today and reap the benefits for years to come.

CHAPTER **11**

Discipline and Tenacity

BECOMING A CORPORATE entrepreneur is a rather unique calling in life. Not everyone is necessarily cut out to face all the challenges that come along with the many rewards. You don't have to be superhuman. However, you do need to possess certain traits and—most importantly—enter the whole corporate entrepreneur lifestyle with a positive mental attitude, and a mindset that is imbued with the right values that are so vital if you want to win at this game. This is something that you need to commit to fully. Going into it halfheartedly is a recipe for disaster.

We are already very familiar with the basics. The idea is to develop side businesses while continuing to work your daytime job that is the centerpiece of your career. By its very definition, the term corporate entrepreneur describes a multifaceted individual who boldly aspires, with dogged determination, to live the American Dream to its utmost potential. Sure, there are many people who are full-time entrepreneurs without a corporate job, and that is a fine and noble way of life too. On the downside, though, their failure rate is much higher because they do not have the financial safety net that you do with your daytime job. If your business is your only source of income, what happens when there are slowdowns or other problems? Your ability to pay basic bills like your mortgage or car payments could be adversely affected. Worrying about these kinds of scenarios adds to your stress level, which as we all know, can be quite harmful to both your physical and mental health. How appropriate that healthcare professionals have labeled stress "the silent killer."

This is not to say that the life of a corporate entrepreneur is not filled with its own challenges. Indeed, there are many of them. However, you will be able to face all of them and overcome the hurdles by cultivating three key traits: Drive, tenacity, and discipline. Let's take a closer look at each of these.

Drive is at the heart of every business endeavor, and it generates the impetus that makes you take the plunge into any new enterprise in the first place; it is what makes you the consummate self-promoter. A properly driven individual is truly unstoppable. You wake up every morning ready to jump out of bed and embrace the brand-new day that presents itself, wide open in front of you. Instead of dreading all the work that you have to do or worrying about what might go wrong, when you are a highly driven person, you view your life and the world that you live in through very different, much more optimistic eyes. You are driven to meet and exceed expectations. Rather than run away from challenges, you see them as opportunities for even more growth and increased success. The drive to continually improve your lot in life is the fuel that keeps you motivated and forever moving forward.

Tenacity is what keeps you single-minded and focused. You have set goals for yourself, and you are determined to accomplish them. It is that little inner voice that keeps urging you to never give up. If you experience a setback or your

DISCIPLINE AND TENACITY

plans don't work out exactly the way you had hoped they would, your tenacity is what will keep you going. A tenacious individual comes to a bump in the road, steels himself for the impact, takes the hit, and then continues on course completely undeterred. Believe me, as a corporate entrepreneur, you are bound to face more than your fair share of bumps in the road. That is why tenacity is so important and so helpful. It pushes you when you feel like you are at your wits' end. It picks you up off the ground when you've taken a fall. And it makes you realize that stumbling blocks and setbacks are not the end of the world. Whatever the challenge is, you are ready for it. Go ahead, obstacles, bring it on! The tenacious corporate entrepreneur is more than prepared and equipped to handle the worst that the world can dish out.

Discipline involves knowing when to say yes and when to say no. It guides you in all your decision-making and guards against impulsiveness. An undisciplined businessperson is headed for one place and one place only: bankruptcy! In all seriousness, without discipline it is impossible to make it in either your daytime career or in any kind of side business. You will aimlessly flounder like a ship without a rudder, always crashing into dangerous reefs and sinking yourself. By sharp contrast, a disciplined man or woman lives by guiding principles that form the bedrock of his or her way of life. Such people never compromise these core beliefs and values—even when strong temptations to do so rear their ugly heads. Never take shortcuts or seek the easy way out. Stay disciplined and do things the right way every time with no exceptions, and in the long run, it will pay out for you in huge dividends.

There are no substitutes for any of these three vital traits. The absence of any of them will all but assure failure. On the other hand, if you possess all three and use them faithfully, diligently, and consistently, you are destined to succeed.

Always keep your eyes open for new business opportunities. Who knows what possibilities might be waiting for you right around the next corner? This means that sometimes you have to make your own breaks, evaluating fresh possibilities at all times. Be self-motivated, first and foremost, and go about everything that you do with an unmatched zeal to succeed.

You also must be the kind of individual who is able to enthusiastically accept and embrace change and new ideas. It can be very helpful to your corporate entrepreneur aspirations if you have witnessed this growing up. People who have been exposed to the concept of working a daytime job, while at the same time engaging in sideline businesses, because that is precisely what they saw their parent or parents doing while they were growing up, should realize with much gratitude, that they are the proud recipients of a unique and invaluable education. That person has somewhat of an advantage moving forward, though such a background is not in any way a prerequisite for you to have your own successful future as a corporate entrepreneur, regardless of your upbringing.

If I may use myself as an example, my father was a European immigrant. I know for a fact that he was the original blueprint, for me, for the whole concept of what it means to be a corporate entrepreneur. He engaged in a number of side businesses while he worked at his full-time machinist job, and he was very successful at both. It's taken me thirty years to accomplish what he was able to achieve in five or ten years in the stock market. He was phenomenal at it, considering that when he first came from Germany he couldn't speak a single word of English.

DISCIPLINE AND TENACITY

While I'm a first-generation son of immigrants, there are many other individuals who have had exposure to grandparents (or other relatives) who have come here with nothing and left behind a legacy of "making it" in America. They've done it in a multitude of vocations in different businesses and activities. The common thread is that everybody learned how to work hard. Tenacity! Nobody had anything given to them. Once they realized that multiple-income streams were indeed possible, they went after that prize with gusto. These ideas are indeed part and parcel of the American fiber, and they go a long way back in our history and traditions.

Nonetheless, most people today are only working at one job to make money—and many of them are just barely getting by. They fail to branch out and open themselves up for other opportunities, because as a full-time employee, they think it is not possible. I grew up learning otherwise. I saw many of my relatives who owned and operated ranches and farms, and at the same time, they also had stores, bars, and restaurants—multiple ways to make money. They had both jobs and family business ventures. The two were in no way ever viewed as mutually exclusive. Witnessing and living amongst such economically diverse individuals has tremendously impacted me and what I do now. As far back as high school, I had it in my head that I was going to be a sales or marketing person, and I was also going to branch out into other side businesses.

For those of you who do not come from that background, no problem. You can still have a successful career as a corporate entrepreneur. The key is getting into businesses that you really enjoy. One example that comes to mind is a colleague of mine who is a big-time car aficionado. He's always buying cars, fixing them up, and selling them. He makes up to $21,000 per month with this side business. This is something that started out as merely a hobby. He does it on evenings and weekends. While maintaining his career in the Big Pharma industry, he never realized that one of his outside interests could become so lucrative.

The lesson here is that opportunity can come to anybody who is watching for it. You can be working successfully at your daytime job and then get into an investment group that opens a franchise restaurant. You never know where your dreams might take you!

Given all this potential, what exactly is it that keeps so many people from venturing out into side businesses? The biggest objection that is self-imposed is "I don't have the time. I'm married, I have kids. I have a busy life." That objection has been squashed by the advent of all the new technology that we have at our fingertips today, such as smart phones. The digital revolution has made organizing your life and communicating worldwide simpler than at any previous time in human history. Take maximum advantage of that!

If you have learned anything about the corporate entrepreneur mentality from this book, you have learned that he or she is a person who is a highly motivated, willing to work hard, a visionary, and someone who is willing to take a few risks. Of course, we're talking about a well-measured risk with a high probability of success. These attributes make the whole game of life so much more enjoyable, satisfying, and meaningful.

CHAPTER **12**

Business Partners

FOR THE CORPORATE entrepreneur, there are both advantages and disadvantages when it comes to the notion of taking on a partner or partners for one or more of your side ventures. And if you do take on a partner, the question inevitably arises: Should it be a full fifty-fifty partnership, where both of you are actively involved in the day-to-day operations of one of your businesses? In general, in most cases my answer would be no. Think about it. There are strong reasons why you don't want another individual to have an equal share of power and control. For starters, at that point, it's not really "your" business anymore, at least not strictly speaking. Moreover, if you are geographically distant from your partner, that tends to hinder your ability to counter any move that he or she might make that does not meet with your approval. Do you really want a partner who can easily challenge and possibly usurp your authority or opinions? This certainly has the potential for creating problems that you clearly don't need.

Bringing in a partner who will own anywhere from 10 to 40 percent makes the most sense, because this way you always maintain control. That would be your best bet. Should a disagreement arise, at least you can rest assured that your view will ultimately prevail.

What is crucial in all of this is making sure that this person is the right fit. It should be someone who is already experienced in the business and has his finger on the pulse of the local competition. In fact, the right person may even come to you *from* the competition. At a bare minimum, you should choose someone who is well versed in the business and highly cognizant of both local circumstances and national trends.

Of course, these traits do not apply to a so-called "silent partner," someone who comes on board strictly from an investor's standpoint. We're not talking about a person who contributes much, if anything, to the day-to-day running of the business, but their infusion of cash can be crucial, especially for a start-up business or a venture that is currently trying to navigate its way through some rough financial waters. Just don't expect them to ease your oversight burdens and responsibilities with the business, because that's not really their function. They're simply looking for a solid return on their investment, and such an arrangement can be beneficial for everyone involved, so long as both parties know and fully understand the boundaries and parameters of their particular roles.

An ideal candidate for a more active partner might be a person who is already managing one of your businesses. General managers often serve well in this capacity. In one of our ventures, the health club business, one of our managers may be going to be buying into the business. He is also going to be elevated to regional manager. These new duties, and his new status as a partial owner, will no doubt open up previously closed doors of opportunity for this ambitious individual. And it will greatly benefit us as well.

When searching for a partner, always seek out someone with complementary skills. For instance, if you're the dealmaker, then the other person would be the one to organize. Or sell. Or maybe he or she would possess some other talent, like the ability to innovate. Whatever the case may be, it is imperative to find a partner who has strength in an area that you are lacking. Ideally, their talents should not mirror yours; rather, they should be in an entirely different area. Or it can even be someone whose talents, while complementing yours, bring a different and valuable perspective. This is especially true if their background is very different from yours.

Remember, one of the concerns that you're always looking to address as a corporate entrepreneur is your limited time. In fact, the biggest reason to have a partner is because this person should have the time available that you might not have at a particular moment. After all, the anchor of all your operations is the day job you hold down that sustains you. It affords you the wherewithal and financial freedom to successfully own and operate your various business enterprises.

An important question that you need to answer early on is: How do you quantify a percentage for a new partner? Every deal is unique. There often may be a certain amount of sweat equity involved. In order for you to properly assess and bestow a part of your business, it needs to be accurately and realistically assessed. The business has to be evaluated, and the most efficient person to do that is your CPA. A specific dollar amount that the partner will receive must be carefully calculated. While being fair to your prospective partner, however, you also need to protect your own interests. There has to be some kind of reduction in value if they quit, which should be tied to their continued employment.

Always watch for red flags, too. For example, they may develop an *ownership* attitude. They might overstep their authority or maybe even try to usurp your authority as the owner. Because they are so close to the business and you are engaged with your day job, they start to imagine that they are really the boss of everything. This type of person develops delusions of grandeur, feeling that the business is actually their own. And you, who are out of sight, might also be out of mind. When that happens, for all practical purposes, you cease being the owner of that business. And that is something that you can never allow to happen!

There is also the temptation and the chance that in a cash-heavy business there are ways to siphon off cash. It is important to screen these potential partners as best as you can. However, nothing you can check can foresee that person getting into trouble, needing money, and figuring out a way to skim it from you. That's one of many reasons why I'm hesitant to run a business that involves a lot of cash. Credit cards are highly preferable. They help to put your mind at ease when it comes to the trust issue. And when you think about it, making your life as a corporate entrepreneur smoother and more efficient—a little peace of mind—is one of your prime motivations for taking on a business partner in the first place.

CHAPTER **13**

Schadenfreude

A CORPORATE ENTREPRENEUR is required to be a very good problem solver. A highly pervasive problem that arises for such an entrepreneur are so-called "toxic people." *Schadenfreude*, a German phrase meaning to enjoy seeing others fail, sums up these particular people well. These types of individuals are often peers or "frenemies." Basic human nature explains the reason why: humans are often jealous of those who possess things that they can't ever have or that they won't even attempt to obtain.

These types of people find their way into every aspect of your business. Some from this group of people will even deliver you bad information when you are seeking a new, physical place for your business. In other words, they will do anything in their power to make your attempts of securing a good geographic location for your business difficult. Perhaps their type of friends or individual interests/beliefs are not compatible with your business ideals, leading these people to seek a way for you to fail. Or maybe, as is often the case, they are simply jealous of your success, ready to do whatever it takes to derail you from achieving your goals.

Such characters have no place in your business; rather, only positive people should be found within your business. However, so-called "yes men" are not the positive kind of people you must seek, because they will try to please you in any way possible, even if that means withholding the truth. A corporate entrepreneur has enough to juggle every single day; thus, these types of people will only drag you down or infringe on the potential success of your business. Understanding this is critical to the success of your business, family, and personal life. Sometimes, cynical people must be fired because of the negative effects they are having on you, even if they are "friends." True friends want you to succeed, and while you should welcome constructive criticism, people who constantly snipe and gripe should be let go, lest their foreboding attitude of gloom and doom becomes a self-fulfilling prophecy.

Therefore, make sure that you select the right person to manage and run your business. The significance and importance of choosing the right person can't be overstated, for it is critical to the success or failure of your business. For example, one who can talk in a polished and informed way, yet does nothing positive or helpful for your business, should not be hired. These people often look for the next way for them to "break big." They think they will win the lottery or become rich by some other fortuitous circumstance such as receiving an unexpected inheritance. Thus, it can be said that these people often believe in the fantasy that they will become rich by some means other than hard (and smart) work. They live in a fantasy world rather than a logical and reality-filled world. Such people should be avoided, as they are often very selfish and full of themselves, which does not bode well for the overall health of your business. Stay away from these toxic people!

Remember, be wary of putting your trust into the wrong person and be aware of people's motives. Such a careful inspection of an individual is needed for both your business and personal life. As has been stated, some people simply want you to fail, for your success somehow threatens them or makes them upset, thus they want to bring you down.

We were looking for a new fitness center in a certain area of the Midwest, and we stumbled upon a person who owned a building from which one of our major competitors in town was leasing. I told him that I was looking on the south side of town and that we were interested in a building. He refused to lease it to us. He wasn't being rational but was not obliged to be otherwise. This was a classic case of business competitors not letting their opposition gain any traction. I was amazed, yet not surprised. We ended up finding a good piece of property in the central south. A grocery store had just gone out of business in this location, and the demographics seemed like a good fit. This was a situation where redoubling our efforts was needed and proved to be successful.

Be cognizant of people in your business who are not looking out for your best interests. They are essentially "business terrorists" seeking for you and your business to fail. The reason why one would do this could be either psychological or perhaps business-related. Maybe they are simply trying to destroy your business because they want to prop up or help another business become successful, or it could just be that they enjoy being aggravating. For example, maybe your general manager is jealous of you and wants to stop you from becoming or continuing to be successful. Such a saboteur will likely hurt themselves at some point, but in the meantime, they find pleasure from hurting you due to their inconsiderate mindset. Whatever the case may be, these kinds of backstabbers should not be working for your business.

This type of person can usually be readily identified, however. More often than not, their true intentions are revealed through a pattern of behaviors which are shown through their interactions with your advocates. Though the revelations may be subtle, you will become aware of their true intentions through their actions, at some point. Be sure that these people are not a part of your business, as they could very well hamper if not outright cripple your efforts.

To avoid all these described complications, see to it that you are a realist rather than an idealist. That is, try not to let folks smooth-talk you, acting like they are positive and respectable people. Some of the most horrible individuals for your business are quite adept at hiding their ulterior motives. Carefully study each person's overall character and history, judging as a realist. Don't be fooled by one who pretends to be positive and great for your business. Realism should overshadow idealism when you set out to hire someone for your business. Remember, sometimes people have great ideas for your business and can talk all day long about it, but they don't act on it. They are simply smooth-talkers, not doers. For example, a relative in my wife's family has a great idea for a business opportunity every few months. But he usually goes into it without giving it his best effort or not pursuing it at all. Doers are needed in your business, not talkers! I apply the three-strike rule to these types of people. After that, I have nothing left to say to them.

I have even had people attempt to borrow money from me to keep their business running. The success of their business is not my responsibility, but rather, theirs. I have to worry about the success of my own business.

SCHADENFREUDE

I had an experience with a toxic person in my business. He was a partner of mine in the potential convenience store business. The result of this person in my business ended badly. In fact, we went all the way to the state's Supreme Court, in a case which I ultimately won. In retrospect (which is the worst way to judge a person), this man failed with every business adventure in which he became involved. In fact, he has not only failed, but he has also been involved with insurance fraud. Therefore, I am quite pleased that we fired him, for he was holding our business back. Such people have no place in one's developing or developed business!

The bottom line? Be super cautious to use good character judgment when trying to select reliable, honest, and trustworthy people for your business. Everybody has a record of achievement or failure; thus, it is important for every potential business associate to be seriously vetted before being chosen to run any part of your business. There is no room for you to become sloppy or lackadaisical when you are selecting someone to help with your business, as such a selection is most important to your success. People whom you don't have daily contact with must be chosen even more carefully than those who do have contact with you daily, because those far away from you can basically go their own way with your business if you let them. Make sure that people you choose to become part of your business team are the complete opposite of a toxic person. They must be reliable, trustworthy, honest, and a great fit for the overall success of your business.

CHAPTER 14

Adapting to New Environments

AN IMPORTANT SKILL that every corporate entrepreneur should master is the ability to become focused, with a certain type of mentality, toward every single one of your business endeavors. In other words, you must be able to adapt to your surroundings. For example, perhaps you want to make a deal with a manufacturer of medical devices in the US. You will want to learn everything you can about that product, as well as the marketing of that product line. It is also important that you learn as much as possible about the company that produces the products. This might require you to think in a way that you seldom do. In other words, you will have to learn the language of the product in question as well as the wording used when selling and marketing it. You must adapt, because that is the only way that you can get into the mindset of each new venture as well as foster the ability to easily switch back and forth from one business to another on any given day.

One of the best ways to learn about a particular product is to contact competitors and ask the kinds of things that a consumer would ask. In all likelihood, they will gladly tell you all sorts of things about their product, hoping that you choose to invest in their product. Doing this will help you become more professional. In fact, we can get great information by calling a competitor's customer service department and asking about their products and services. Every industry has an 800 number and a website. These are wonderful means of gaining valuable knowledge about virtually any company.

We also sometimes call a company and realize that a competitor is actually superior to us and that they too don't yet have a distributor. Perhaps this is a good time to go with them. This is how we got together with the hydrocolloid company. We discovered that some of the products of the company we were working with were made by their competitor. Interestingly enough, we soon ended up working with them.

Remember the old saying "When in Rome, do as the Romans do"? Well, if people in a certain industry wear high-end suits and ties, then you should too. If they wear sweater vests, wear sweater vests. Simply put, adapt to the way that they dress and wear clothes that they would most likely wear. By doing this, you will be able to go to their home office, playing the part. You will increase your chances of getting a contract with them, becoming a distributor for their company.

You don't have to change who you are, but it is necessary to be flexible in how you present yourself—not only your appearance but also your overall demeanor and the words that you use—in order to conform to any particular industry. Simply put, you must learn the culture of a certain business with which you want to become involved. Even learning how they pay their representatives, your future work associates, is important in order for you to succeed.

Become knowledgeable about the audience you are targeting, right away. Just like with any new business or venture, you must have a business plan. Make sure that you show them the direction that you will be taking, and convince these people that you will be successful, as you confidently move things forward. In fact, we have done that with every business that we have represented. Furthermore, we have interviewed people in that industry in order to educate ourselves in their field.

Another example of a way in which we had to adapt is when we were getting ready to build the storage complex. We went to all the seminars and meetings, and we started behaving like the owner of a storage complex. We didn't wear suits and ties. We wore cowboy boots, jeans, and plain jackets. This is the way that we recalibrated ourselves in that business.

Whatever the case may be, you need to learn that industry's lingo, terms, and even their attitudes. My wife, for example, came from the area of interior design, having done fancy decorating and some party planning. She ended up becoming the manager of our storage complex for about seven years. To fit well with the business, she had to completely retrain herself. That is just another benefit of having someone close to you, work with you, and provide a real boost to your corporate entrepreneurial efforts. Overall, she always went the extra step to learn as much as she could.

When seeking to receive a representation contract, your presentation is the most important part in your attempt at making the deal. You are now becoming a distributor for that company and building a strong rapport with them. Presumably, you have already made the phone calls, gone on Skype, and have attended dinner with them. By this point, you are ready to complete a contract.

So, you have a complete process that you follow. After you have used all your effort to win them over, you will know you did an excellent job if they are talking about putting together a contract.

Keep in mind that there isn't just one thing that you must do in order to impress them. There is a whole series of steps that must be followed to make them feel comfortable with your talents as well as your people. Bringing in your "wing man" (your business partner or trusted associate) to these negotiations is, more often than not, a wise and very helpful move.

Be careful about the "order of things." It is better to underpromise and overdeliver than it is to do the reverse. In fact, I have overpromised and then underdelivered before. It was a painful experience.

We once dealt with a company that did light therapy; it would basically go on a person's face to increase their collagen, thus tightening the skin on their face. We badly misjudged the market and thought we could sell more than we did. In four or five months, we realized that our sales projections were very far off. However, we also got involved with other medical products (involving nerve pain), and we were much more successful with them. Don't expect to hit it out of the park every time. Just be sure to learn something from every "at bat" that you take.

Can all the juggling from one business to the next get confusing? Of course it can! I'd get calls about my storage complex, and then I would talk to someone about the health care industry. I would also be going into a lecture for my day job in the pharma business. Nevertheless, with practice and experience, you will get used to it.

Trust me: Don't be scared off by thinking that this will be too difficult. Once you've been at it for a while, all this will become second nature to you. As a matter of fact, there will come a day when you find it hard to imagine not living the always eventful, and certainly never boring, lifestyle of a corporate entrepreneur.

CHAPTER **15**

Lessons Learned

HAVING LIVED THE life of a corporate entrepreneur for thirty years, I've picked up some valuable lessons along the way. Sure, there have been some obstacles and problems, but overall, it is remarkable how very positive my experiences have been over these past three decades. Even the people I've associated with have for the most part been quite supportive. There were only a few people along the way who tried to trip me up.

When we were the principal in these businesses, and I was the majority owner (or my wife and I were), we were always more successful. We have never faced any major roadblocks. It seems as though our own ideas were the best. Obviously, we may have had silent or less involved partners, but we never shared the power of a business fifty-fifty with a partner. We always wanted to have more say in the business than any other partner. There was only one exception: when I had a fifty-fifty partnership with a good friend of mine, from the Big Pharma industry, in the medical field. Because he was a good friend of mine, from within my "day job" industry, the relationship was more easily equitable and fair, with few arguments. However, I still hold that you should strive to be the principal of a business, though I realize that this is not always possible.

Someone may ask whether my primary day job ever suffered because of my many side businesses. The answer is no, it did not. Even when I was most involved with my sideline businesses, my primary day job did not suffer. This is because I was always an independent marketer and salesperson and was on the road, being my own boss and manager. I was never chained to a desk. If I were deskbound, I may have had a different experience.

If you ever feel like you can't get ahead in your primary day job, realize that you are doing much better than your colleagues, no matter what their career path is, because you are in effect leading a double life. A friend of mine has the same day job as me but is in the process of starting a campaign for the US Congress. To me, that is his side venture, and I have a lot of respect for what he is doing because he will face many of the same challenges that corporate entrepreneurs deal with on a daily basis.

Of course, all this depends on the nature of your side businesses. If you have bad management in your side businesses, I can see how you might have problems that could distract from a day job. Such would have been the case for me if I had bad management in my side businesses.

To me, the most important characteristic to have, to do what I do, is discipline. If you do not have the discipline, and things are becoming too much of a hassle, then the corporate entrepreneur lifestyle is simply not for you. If you can't chew gum and dribble a basketball, so to speak, then it is not for you.

There are ways to see if being a corporate entrepreneur is for you. You can start some test businesses. Take real estate development, for example. Being in such a business does not take a lot of hands-on effort. You may ultimately build office buildings or medical buildings or maybe strip malls. Overall, remember that the locations of these businesses are very important.

Some people have asked me, "How does operating sideline business ventures affect your retirement plan?" It all depends. You want to make an exit strategy for these sideline businesses. For example, there are people who are interested in buying our storage complex. We have owned it for fifteen years, and it is probably worth ten or twelve times more than what the average person has in their 401k. In fact, I have an exit strategy for all my properties.

The formula for the sale price of most businesses is as follows: we take the gross sales and multiply it by two and a half.

The largest holding of ours is our health and fitness business. We are probably going to sell part of them to the general manager of the existing business.

Of course, there are also some people who enjoy retiring from their day job and spending time managing their side businesses.

There are lots of different approaches that you can take. Your main goal is to make sure that your family is comfortable and that there is a legacy of wealth for you to pass on. In many cases, the money flows from one generation to the next. Another goal to keep in mind is to get your businesses paid off as soon as possible.

In sum, one thing that I didn't know when I first started was the tremendous importance of hiring the right people. That is a true game-changer. You also need to keep in mind with whom you reveal your business plans. Be especially cautious about revealing your plans to your coworkers. I have had some colleagues, for example, who were extremely envious, and even VPs and GMs who were insanely envious. Well, I was making five times as much as them, so I guess that explains it! If I had known about their envy, I would have been more careful about sharing certain concepts with them. There is a reason why you have two ears and one mouth.

My hope, of course, is that as you set out on your own path to become a corporate entrepreneur, you will learn from my experiences, and some day will look back on your career and smile with satisfaction that you took that little step of faith, to believe in yourself enough to do things in a different way—a better way, which leads to a better life for you and your family—the life of the corporate entrepreneur..

www.ingramcontent.com/pod-product-compliance
Lightning Source LLC
Chambersburg PA
CBHW020442220526
45464CB00002B/818